ALEXANDER CRUMMELL

Alexander Crummell, 1819-1898. Photo courtesy of Moorland-Springarn Research Center, Howard University.

ALEXANDER CRUMMELL

Pioneer in Nineteenth-Century Pan-African Thought

Gregory U. Rigsby

Foreword by Arthur P. Davis

Contributions in Afro-American
and African Studies, Number 101

GREENWOOD PRESS

NEW YORK • WESTPORT, CONNECTICUT • LONDON

Library of Congress Cataloging-in-Publication Data

Rigsby, Gregory U.
  Alexander Crummell : pioneer in nineteenth-century
Pan-African thought.

  (Contributions in Afro-American and African studies,
ISSN 0069-9624 ; no. 101)
  Bibliography: p.
  Includes index.
  1. Crummell, Alexander, 1819-1898. 2. Afro-Americans
—Biography. 3. Pan-Africanism—History—19th century.
I. Title. II. Series.
E185.97.C87R54 1987   973'.0496073'0924 [B] 86-15034
ISBN 0-313-25570-9 (lib. bdg. : alk. paper)

Library of Congress Catalog Card Number: 86-15034
ISBN: 0-313-25570-9
ISSN: 0069-9624

First published in 1987

Greenwood Press, Inc.
88 Post Road West, Westport, Connecticut 06881

Printed in the United States of America

∞

The paper used in this book complies with the
Permanent Paper Standard issued by the National
Information Standards Organization (Z39.48-1984).

10 9 8 7 6 5 4 3 2 1

To My Wife and Children
Babs, Kwema, Drina, and Bita

and

To My Mentors
Dr. Arthur P. Davis
Dr. Ivan E. Taylor

Contents

Foreword

This scholarly and pioneering study on Alexander Crummell by Gregory Rigsby tells us a great deal about every aspect of the life of this remarkable man, but it is by no means a conventional biography. Going far beyond the limits of the usual life–and–works narrative, Dr. Rigsby depicts the growth, the maturation, the making of his subject; he shows in depth the historical, religious, educational, and racial forces which helped to shape Crummell and which in turn were influenced by him. In short, Rigsby has presented to the reader a penetrating and unusual fusing of man and age. The first of its kind on Crummell, this treatise is a timely and highly needed reappraisal of a great scholar–leader who should be far better known than he is.

Though never completely forgotten, Crummell has had no major place in black history texts or literary anthologies and, of course, no previous significant biographical treatment. And yet this man was a classical scholar when there were few if any other Blacks in that field; he was a dynamic church leader and builder, a well–known and controversial missionary, an innovative and effective educator, and a Christian mystic; he was above all else a seminal figure who foreshadowed leaders as diverse as Booker T. Washington, W.E.B. Du Bois, and Marcus Gravey.

In short, Alexander Crummell, as this treatise so brilliantly demonstrates, was one of the truly great black intellectual leaders of the nineteenth century.

Rigsby's study is perhaps more relevant and pertinent now than it would have been if produced earlier. We have experienced the revolution of the 1960s, and as a consequence we understand better and have a deeper appreciation of this pioneer thinker who promulgated the basic ideas and tenets of the Black Revolution, among them: emphasis on Africa as the homeland, the glorification of blackness, and the oneness of all the far-flung sons of Africa, wherever they may be. It should be therapeutic for young black scholars to learn that not all of their principles were generated in the 1960s.

In this comprehensive analysis of Crummell and his times, the author throws new light on many of Crummell's well-known contemporaries like Edward Blyden, Paul Cuffe, Peter Williams, Jr., Henry Highland Garnet, Martin R. Delany, and others. In their contact with Alexander Crummell, these figures often show qualities, good and questionable, not found in other works on them.

Though a scholarly work, this treatise is by no means dull or stuffy. It has many fascinating and intriguing vignettes describing the bickering and feuding among black missionary-churchmen, the governmental failures in Liberia, the prejudice of some of the white clergymen who headed boards and committees concerned with black ministers, the segregation and discrimination which all Negroes of the period found in the "Free" North, the virulent animosity between light-colored (mulatto) Negroes and blacks. These pictures of all-too-human men in high positions give a freshness not often found in scholarly works.

Alexander Crummell, like Du Bois, his intellectual heir, was an extremely complex and paradoxical person—at times petty, at times saintly. Also like

Dr. Du Bois, he seemed to be constantly changing his position on significant issues. On one day he would emphasize the supreme importance of a practical education for Negroes; on another he would insist that high intellectual and classical training was a necessity for black advancement. Nevertheless, again like Du Bois, he could and did justify brilliantly each position taken, no matter how inconsistent it appeared at first blush. The reader, however, soon realizes that all of Crummell's seeming vacillation was grounded on the unchanging bedrock of a deep and mystical faith.

The product of an incredible amount of scholarly research and an equal amount of devotion to the author's subject, this treatise makes an invaluable contribution to the literature of the nineteenth century, particularly as it concerns Negroes. Dr. Rigsby has returned to us a great intellectual leader, perhaps the greatest prior to Du Bois; he has rescued Alexander Crummell from that state of semi-oblivion in which he has been, and has placed him where he belongs, among the seminal pioneer black intellectuals who gave direction to the course of black life in America.

Arthur P. Davis

Prologue

In his classic *The Souls of Black Folk*, W.E.B. Du
Bois wrote concerning Alexander Crummell: "His
name today, in this broad land, means little, and
comes . . . with no incense of . . . emulation . . .
herein lies the tragedy of the age."[1] Many scholars
have acknowledged the tremendous influence the
Reverend Crummell had on nineteenth-century life in
black America and West Africa,[2] and several
intellectuals who knew Crummell personally have
testified, in their published writings, to Crummell's
magnificent physical presence and his brilliant intellectual acumen.[3] However, to date there is no full-
length biographical study of Alexander Crummell.

To say that this study is the definitive biography
of Crummell is too ambitious. This study will limit its
focus to Crummell's Pan-African ideas and his
spiritual approach to life. "Pan-African" in this study
means the unification of all Africans and people of
African descent. More specifically, it means racial
solidarity among black people and native Africans.[4]
It will be seen that, for Crummell, Pan-Africanism
was not an end in itself but a short-term goal toward
the larger aim of human unity. He sought through his
Pan-African program to uplift the black race from its
condition of servitude. Crummell's spiritual approach
to life was characterized by a heightened awareness

of a transcendental order in this world "where men sit and hear each other groan." This spiritual awareness was cultivated and nurtured by his Christian upbringing and his rigorous Episcopal training.

Born free in New York City on March 3, 1819, Crummell studied at Cambridge University in England, ministered to black people in Africa for twenty years, and finally returned to America to live the last twenty-five years of his life. He died peacefully on September 10, 1898, in Dr. Matthew Anderson's summer home in Point Pleasant, New Jersey. Thus, Crummell's life conveniently falls into four distinct periods: (1) 1819–1847: his training in America; (2) 1847–1853: his education in England; (3) 1853–1873: his missionary work in Africa; and (4) 1873–1898: his final years of influence in America.

The framework for Crummell's Pan–African ideas and spiritual attitudes was established in his youth. Thus, the first chapter examines the various influences on Crummell's Pan–African ideas, traces his academic and religious training, and offers a close reading of his early writings. In this first phase of Crummell's life, his major Pan–African concern was group solidarity among black Americans, with the talented and educated black people having the responsibility to pull up the masses of the black race. In the second chapter, which deals with his stay in England, attention is paid to Crummell's broadened concerns for a more international Pan–Africanism as expressed in his many speeches. The third chapter, centered in Liberia, is pivotal to this study. A close analysis is given of Crummell's efforts to make Liberia a Pan–African nation under the umbrella of the Christian faith. His dream became a nightmare, and, based on his Liberian experiences, he realized that the moving force to raise the race was the untutored masses of native Africans. The fourth and final chapter discusses the various ways Crummell sought to bring his newfound belief in the black masses to post–Reconstruction America. His Pan–African concept returned to the consolidation of black Americans, and he proposed service as the defining quality of any true Pan–Africanist. Underlying all phases of Crummell's Pan–African concepts was a fervent belief that intellectual and moral excellence must be the foundation for any meaningful black unity. As an elderly man, Crummell still cherished the spiritual capacities of black people, and even on his deathbed, he expressed a deep faith that, in the end, "We shall overcome."

Acknowledgments

I thank the many persons who have helped me in getting this work done: The staffs of the Schomburg Library and the Moorland–Spingarn Room at Howard University, and especially the librarian, Margaret Dorsey, formerly of the University of the District of Columbia, who assisted me in locating and obtaining material through interlibrary loans. I would also like to express my special gratitude to V. Nelle Bellamy, archivist for the Archives of the Episcopal Church in Austin, Texas; F. G. Ranney, archivist for the Maryland Diocesan Archives, who voluntarily helped to transcribe illegibly written letters, guided me to biographical information on Episcopal ministers, and informed me about significant historical events in the Episcopal Church of the Washington Metropolitan area; Dorothy Owen, archivist at the University of Cambridge, who responded promptly to my inquiries concerning Crummell's activities while he attended the University of Cambridge; J. Carleton Hayden of Morgan State University, who served as my sponsor to the archives at Texas, gave me invaluable bibliographical assistance, and directed me to others who might be working on Alexander Crummell; Russell Adams and Arthur P. Davis of Howard University, who read early drafts of my work and suggested stylistic and structural changes; my colleague, Mary

Martin, who helped with editing, proofreading, indexing, and bibliographical suggestions; Kwema Rigsby, my daughter, who helped with proofreading and word processing; Joyce Rose, who typed early drafts of the study; and my wife and children for their support and encouragement.

ALEXANDER CRUMMELL

1

Alexander Crummell's Training in America

The earliest influence on Alexander Crummell's thinking was his father, Boston Crummell. From his father Crummell adopted the ruling thoughts of his life—Africa, race, and aristocracy. Young Crummell first heard about Africa from his father, who used to tell him tales about the kingdom of Timmanee in West Africa from which he (Boston) was stolen when he was about twelve or thirteen years old. Alexander learned with pride that his grandfather was chief of the Timmanee people, and that his own father was a prince who often received gifts and royal treatment whenever he accompanied his father on his "royal tours." So vividly and with such "burning love of home" would Boston Crummell recall scenes and customs of various tribes in Africa, that young Crummell had resolved to go to "the land of our fathers" at the first opportunity he had.[1] It is irrelevant whether Boston Crummell was truly a prince or not; the fact is his son believed it and was fond of recounting his royal lineage to his friends.[2] This belief that his father was a prince affected Crummell deeply, for throughout his life he believed in the inheriting of "royal blood." In the eulogy of his dear friend Henry Highland Garnet, he made much of a legend concerning Garnet's inheriting royal African blood from his grandfather, who was imputed to be a

Mandingo chieftain warrior. Referring to this claim of chieftainship for Garnet, Crummell commented, "the fires of liberty were never quenched in the blood of his family." Thus when Crummell heard that his grandparents were of royal lineage, he evidently tried to live up to the African reputation of his Temne* tribe. The Temne chief was regarded as "a benign individual" who was surrounded with a "mystical, supernatural aura."[3] The descriptions of Crummell by people who knew him personally were always descriptions of someone majestic and stately in bearing, and commanding, if not superior, in mind. Professor William Ferris, the author of *The African Abroad*, characterized him as "a born autocrat . . . [before whom] men instinctively bowed." William Wells Brown described him as "a tall and manly figure, commanding in appearance, [with] a full and musical voice, fluent in speech." The Reverend Henry L. Phillips, a close friend and admirer of Crummell who later became an active Garveyite, pictured him as, "tall, erect, dignified, highly cultured, black and the quintessence of neatness." Throughout his seventy-nine years, he maintained high moral values, and, indeed the only fault one of his ex-pupils from Liberia who had become a high political figure in the Liberian government could offer about his mentor was: "He was a little too rigid."[4] Even William Wells Brown tended to fault Crummell for being "too punctilious," though he admitted that Crummell lived what he asked of others. There was, without doubt, something princely about this great black man who was ever proud of his pure African ancestry.

From his mother's way of life as wife and mother in the household, Crummell learned the deep respect for womanhood which he displayed throughout his life. "It is the women," he wrote much later in his

---

*Temne is a spelling variation of Timmanee.

life, "who gave the sap to every human organization which thrives and flourishes on earth."[5] Crummell's mother, whose maiden name was Charity Hicks, was not a native African; she was born a free black woman of unmixed African blood in the state of New York. Crummell did not write much about her, and no notice of her name can be found in any of the black publications or letters of the day, and except in Walter B. Hayson's eulogy before the American Negro Academy in 1898, there is no mention of her name in the many eulogies for her famous son. Crummell did acknowledge that she was a shaping influence on his life: "How much she was to me! What great things she did for me! If we would only all our days think, day-by-day, about our mothers, what noble and exalted men we'd always be."[6] His mother's self-effacement but strong support for her husband and children became Crummell's measuring rod for black wives and mothers.

The compassionate concern that Crummell expressed for the post-Reconstruction black woman of the South, and his insistence that women be an integral part of any Pan-African nation-building effort in Liberia were the result, at least in part, of the observations he made as a young boy of his mother's firm support of her husband and the disciplined but loving home she maintained. Praising, in general, the black woman's "sweetness of disposition and deep humility, . . . unselfish devotedness, and . . . warm, motherly assiduities," he offered as personal testimony "the memory of my own mother."[7] Crummell held her in reverence throughout his life, and when he was experiencing exceedingly difficult times as a missionary in Africa, still he brought his mother, an elderly woman well into her eighties, to live with him in the comfort of his home and to die peacefully in the land of her ancestors within a few miles from where her husband was born.

In conjunction with Crummell's father and mother,

the Reverend Peter Williams, Jr., touched Crummell's life directly. Crummell's first schooling was at Peter Williams's school on Cliff Street where he was taught Latin and Greek[8] and Williams once provided Crummell with money to enable him to continue his schooling.[9] Moreover, Williams later urged the teenage Crummell to challenge the racial policies of the General Theological Seminary under the director-ship of Bishop Benjamin T. Onderdonk, and Crummell himself, as an old man, in his Jubilate address publicly acknowledged Williams as having a profound influence on his life.

Indeed, Crummell's Pan–African consciousness developed significantly at the feet of Peter Williams. Pan–Africanism for Peter Williams was no ideological quest; it was a living reality. His mother was a "lady of color" from the West Indies; his father, whose parents were brought from Africa as slaves, was of pure African stock; and Peter, Jr., was himself a second–generation Afro–American. Africa was no dream of the mystical past for Peter Williams; it was the home of his grandparents, and he grew up learn-ing much about African customs from his grand-parents and his father. Undoubtedly, the strong African background in his own family which Crum-mell conspicuously wore throughout his life, coupled with his pastor's (the Reverend Mr. Williams's) African lineage which included a colored West Indian presence, helped to direct Crummell's mind along Pan–African pathways.

In his famous *An Oration on the Abolition of the Slave Trade* (1808),[10] Williams promoted the kind of Pan–African thinking that later saturated the soul of Crummell. Speaking to an Afro–American audience, Williams transcended geographical and national lines and saw all black people as Africans. His speech was sprinkled with expressions such as "to us Africans and descendants of Africans,"[11] and, as if to dispel any doubt as to whom he was referring, he

appealed, "Let . . . the heart that is warmed by the
smallest drop of African blood glow."[12] Crummell
never abandoned this broad and all-inclusive
definition of a black person even during his bitterest
conflicts with mulattoes in Liberia and in
Washington, D.C. This definition carried with it a
proud assertion of the black race and counteracted
any tendency among black people to define their race
in terms of the fraction of white blood that might be
coursing through their veins. Crummell did not
hesitate, however, to exclude from his Pan-African
community any black person who did not eagerly
embrace his African ancestry.

Besides providing Crummell with ideas for "blood
brotherhood," Williams also reinforced the burning
love for Africa that Boston Crummell had instilled
into his son's breast. Williams shared Paul Cuffe's
dream about Africa.[13] He was Cuffe's main contact for the African Institution which Cuffe had
established in New York in order to pursue the idea
of colonization and emigration to Africa.[14] Cuffe,
indeed, recommended Williams as one of his key
supporters in his African plan to set up a mercantile
line of business between Africa and the United
States, and there is record of Williams's having
recruited a carpenter in New York to go to Sierra
Leone.[15] This link between Cuffe and Williams would
never be broken. In his 1817 eulogy on Paul Cuffe,
Williams argued that Cuffe was "truly great": He had
settled black Americans in Sierra Leone at a personal
cost of about $3,000 to $4,000; and he felt that
colonization was not only workable but the best step
for Afro-Americans to take. With this understanding Williams exhorted, "Let us not . . . hastily
condemn a measure [the colonization of Africa] to
which every fibre of his [Cuffe's] heart clung."[16]
Though by 1830 Williams had rejected colonization,
he still held on to the spirit of Cuffe's dream by
encouraging black American missionaries to emigrate

to Africa. In this very eulogy, Williams solicited help for the Canadian settlement of the expelled black people of Cincinnati. He made a distinction between voluntary and involuntary emigration: "This scheme of colonization [Canadian] . . . has originated among our own people. It is not of the devising of the white men."[17] The step to voluntary emigration to Africa was not difficult to take.

According to Williams, Cuffe's African scheme was founded on his basic identification with his race. Cuffe was not interested in separating black America from Africa, in settling some black people in Africa and then forgetting those who remained in America. Williams was particularly impressed with this Pan-African thinking of Cuffe's and noted it in his eulogy: "Considering himself (to use his own phraseology) as a member of the whole African family he was unwilling to leave that part of it which was in America."[18] Williams was deeply moved by the devotion and generosity of Paul Cuffe to the black race. He quotes xhim as saying, "My wish . . . is for the good of this people universally."[19] It is this kind of racial solidarity thinking that was to pass from Cuffe to Williams to Crummell to Du Bois and Garvey, to Malcolm X. The energy of this line of thinking is generated by putting the group before the individual; it is the submerging of personal likes to the communal welfare; it is putting the racial family before self. Williams was careful to point out that Cuffe had explained in a letter the reason he had established the African Institutions in New York and Philadelphia: "[so that] the colored people of these large cities would be more awakened than from an individual."[20] Though the sentence syntax is somewhat awkward, the meaning is clear. Cuffe was not interested in black Americans settling in Africa so that they, as individuals, might enjoy a better life, as those first emigrants he had transported sought, but in order that they might bring to the indigenous peoples whatever skills and knowledge they had acquired in America, and so that they in turn might develop their genius free from the stifling racial prejudices in America. In this way, Cuffe hoped (with Williams's assent) that the black race would lift itself. It was this Pan–African ideal of Cuffe that Williams never abandoned even after he stood up to the American Colonization Society.

These early influences on his thinking created in Crummell an African consciousness. Like many other black Americans of that age, Crummell thought of himself as African. This is an important point, because what one conceives oneself to be carries more weight than where one happens to be born. James McCune Smith, the Scottish–trained black physician, attests that, "The people [Afro–Americans and West Indians] in those days [the 1820s] . . . hesitated not to call each other 'Africans.'"[21] It was not until 1835, at a National Negro Convention, that the assembly voted to drop the term "African" from the name of black associations.[22] This action was political strategy to fight against what free Blacks saw as a deportation plan under the guise of an African colonization scheme. But one cannot change what one conceives oneself to be by vote. The descriptive title might be different, but the self–concept remains the same. It must be remembered also that there were still many African–born Blacks in America during the early decades of the nineteenth century.[23] Thus, the dropping of the term "African" might help to build a case against deporting free Blacks to Africa, but it certainly could not abruptly stop black people like Crummell from thinking of themselves as "African."

Yet Crummell saw the need to stand up for his rights as an American citizen. The American Colonization Society (ACS), which had stated as its purpose the setting up of a colony in Africa peopled with black American volunteers,[24] had launched a propaganda campaign representing black people as degraded and licentious and a nuisance to be gotten rid of.[25] As a result of this propaganda, racial prejudice increased to the point that in 1829 the infamous expulsion laws of Cincinnati were put into effect, and all free black people of that city had to leave, lock, stock and barrel, and emigrate to Canada. It is one thing for a person to choose to go home, but it is quite another matter to be asked to leave. As much as Crummell, or any black American, might think of himself as African and might wish to return to his African homeland, the fact is he has the right to remain in America if he so chooses. And Crummell was determined to exercise this right to stay.

His mentor, Peter Williams, underscored in Crummell's mind the need for every black American to claim his rights as an American citizen. In the early years of the ACS, Williams had appealed to black Americans to suspend judgment of the ACS "until we see further development."[26] After the Cincinnati debacle, however, Williams, in an eloquent address in 1830 at St. Phillip's Church, condemned the cruel acts meted out against his brothers in Ohio in order to force "all the free coloured people of the United States, to the distant shores of Africa."[27] No longer was Williams asking his audience to suspend judgment; he was explicitly condemning African colonization. The Africa that Williams had romanticized in his 1808 oration celebrating the abolition of the slave trade in New York ("thy shores which were once the garden of the world, the sea of almost paradisical joys")[28] was now transformed in this 1830 address into a hostile Africa ("the burning sun, the arid plains, and barbarous customs of Africa").[29]

It was not that black Americans wanted to obliterate their Africanness so much as they resented being callously discarded as aliens who needed to be deported. Here was a people whose foreparents had slaved to build this nation and whose brethren (often literally speaking) were currently slaving to make this country cotton–rich; here was a people whose foreparents had fought and died to help make this country free and independent and some of whom themselves might have been recently enlisted into the two regiments of black troops that had been recruited to fight in the War of 1812; here was a people who in the face of racial discrimination in all aspects of society (political, religious, economic, educational, and social) yet kept their faith and tried to be loyal and law–abiding citizens; and here were these people, born and bred on American soil, being literally pushed aside so that European whites could become the skilled labor force of the nation. These foreigners who in no way participated in the building of America—in fact, many of whose foreparents had fought against this country—were being encouraged and welcomed into these lands now that the American nation was on the upswing. This was an intolerable state of affairs, and black people were cut to the quick about it. As spokesman for the deep hurt that black people felt, the Reverend Peter Williams displayed restraint, dignity, and eloquence:

> We are natives of this country, we ask only to be treated as well as foreigners. Not a few of our fathers suffered and bled to purchase its independence; we ask only to be treated as well as those who fought against it. We have toiled to cultivate it, and to raise it to its present prosperous condition; we ask only to share equal privileges with those who came from distant lands to enjoy the fruits of our labor. Let these moderate requests be granted, and we need not go to Africa nor anywhere else, to be improved and happy.[30]

Four years later, Williams reiterated his attack on the ACS: "Far be it for us to forget or slight the kindness of some who have urged upon us the plan of colonization, but they must not now stand in our way for a better and further advancement in the land of [our] birth."[31] When Williams had described African customs as being "barbarous" and had recommended that, "A few well-qualified missionaries . . . would do more for the . . . improvement of the natives of [Liberia] . . . than a host of Colonists,"[32] he represented the kind of Pan-African relationship black leaders were sowing in the minds of young Blacks like Crummell. Cuffe, too, had seen this Pan-African union as a one-way effort by black Americans who had to "pull up," as it were, native Africans to their westernized standard of living. Crummell's earliest Pan-African concept will follow this line of thinking, and only after he had lived several years in Africa did he shift from this "pull from the top" to the "push from below" approach to Pan-African unity.

When Crummell was eight years old, a significant event occurred at his house. On March 16, 1827, famous black people like Samuel Cornish, an alumnus of the African Free School, and John Russwurm, then thought to be the first black person to graduate from an American college (in fact, he was the second black person to graduate),[33] met at Boston Crummell's house and founded the first black newspaper in America, *Freedom's Journal*. The African Free School which Crummell attended subscribed to the paper, and several years later, when the paper had changed its name to *Colored American*, Crummell became an agent for the paper and had his first piece of published writing appear in its pages. Without a doubt, Crummell read the newspaper and was exposed to the ideas expressed in its pages.

In the pages of *Freedom's Journal* was dramatized a dilemma that Alexander Crummell had to face—"the double-consciousness" of the black American—being American and African at the same time. In issue after issue of the black newspaper, Africa and Africans were being extolled, yet the thrust of the paper was to discourage African colonization and encourage American thinking among the black populace—to embrace Africa in one arm and claim America with the other. When, for example, an Egyptian mummy was put on display in New York, the *Journal* took the opportunity to claim Egypt as being part of black Africa, via Herodotus.[34] Again, a comparative study between Egyptian and American slavery appeared in the June 29 paper, and in this very issue, after stating explicitly that "the Egyptian and African are one people," a feature article sought to show how "the people of China should be considered as a colony of Egyptians." Achievements of other black people outside of America were also played up in the pages of the newspaper.

Despite all this pride in Africa, no one could miss the vigorous opposition the *Journal* took against colonization. When Henry Clay spoke at an annual meeting of the ACS, a lengthy comment on the speech was made in the May 18 issue of the *Journal*, with special emphasis on a quote from Mr. Clay's speech: "It [the ACS] is to have nothing to do with the delicate question of slavery." The free black population, however, had a deeper interest in emancipation than colonization. The *Journal* conceded that the Liberian colony could serve well as "a missionary station, a home for recaptured Africans,* or an Asylum for such slaves as their masters . . . emancipate," but always would the paper insist that free black Americans had rights "as good as any other free citizens."[35] Even after Samuel Cornish announced his resignation as co-editor of the *Journal*, and John Russwurm who eventually capitulated to the ACS began representing procolonizationists' views in the newspaper,[36] still the *Journal* published anticolo-

---

*A term used to describe Africans who were liberated from slave ships bound for the New World.

nizationist sentiments such as those expressed by Bishop Richard Allen, the preeminent black leader of the era: "This land which we have watered with *our tears* and *our blood* is now our *mother country* and we are well satisfied to stay [here]."

Boston Crummell also represented this dilemma to his son. The senior Crummell would fill his son's imagination with tales of regal life in Africa, yet it is reputed that Boston Crummell led the delegation that angrily demanded the resignation of John Russwurm as editor of *Freedom's Journal* for capitulating to the views of the ACS and choosing to live in Africa rather than in America.[37] Many a black man in America still longed for his African homeland and African brethren, but he was adamant on his right to live in America.

But was the question really: Can an African be also an American? The crux of the problem lay on the American side of the equation. Granted his right to live in America, should a black person *choose* to live in America? Given legal citizenship, could a black person ever realistically hope to become a full-fledged American citizen? After all, unlike other immigrants, the African was involuntarily brought to America and treated inhumanely within the slave system. Can the black man ever sufficiently forget the exploitation he suffered as slave and even as freedman to become part of the American family? And on the other hand, will white Americans ever surrender the legacy of their feelings of superiority bred by slavery, to be able to accept the black man as a fellow citizen? James McCune Smith spoke of the hope; John Russwurm sounded the note of despair. Smith, characterizing the mood of black people in the early decades of the nineteenth century, asserted, "The colored people of New York, from an early date, carried themselves with a free air . . . [and] felt themselves free."[38] Russwurm, in his parting editorial (1829), painted a bleak future for black people in America: "In the bosom of the most enlightened community upon the globe, we are ignorant and degraded; under the most republican government, we are denied all the rights and privileges of citizens; and what is still worse, we see no probability, that we as a community will ever make it . . . to rise from our ignorance and degradation."[39]

On a personal level the ten-year-old Crummell grappled with this "black American dilemma." In 1829, the very year Russwurm sailed for Liberia, Crummell witnessed a scene that remained etched indelibly on his mind throughout his life. His schoolmate and closest friend, Henry Highland Garnet, had to leave school to work as a cabin boy on a schooner. While Garnet was away, Crummell saw one of those hated men who earned a living by capturing black people who had escaped slavery and returning them to that disgusting institution. This "slave-catcher" had traced the whereabouts of the Garnet family, "his former property," but could not recognize that the majestic, overbearing black man who now stood in his presence was the "slave" he sought. Mr. Garnet, on the other hand, quickly recognized his former owner and leaving the sick-souled slave hunter at the door, he cleverly excused himself under the pretext of seeking out the person who was asked for. What happened next Crummell described as he saw it: "The opened window was about twenty feet from the ground; between the two houses was an alley at least four feet wide; the only way of escape was to leap from the side window . . . how [Mr. Garnet] escaped breaking both neck and legs is a mystery to me to this day."[40] This, in New York, where men by law were free! Freedom, young Crummell realized, did not mean for black people a life of liberty to pursue life's goals as they saw fit. The subsequent dispersal of the Garnet family and the bitterness engendered in the breast of the teenage Henry Highland Garnet when he learned of the fate of his family demon-

strated to Crummell grounds for Russwurm's pessi-
mistic outlook for black people living in America and
the justification for his option to emigrate to Africa.
It was in 1829, too, one must remember, that the
explusion of the Cincinnati black people took place.
Yet, it was in this same year that Peter Williams and
Boston Crummell stiffened their resolve to fight for
their rights to be full-fledged American citizens,
and, in the following year, Crummell experienced an
episode that might pass as trivial, but that played a
significant part in giving direction to his life. While
working in an antislavery office in New York, Crummell overheard John C. Calhoun's comment on the
inability of the Negro to conjugate a Greek verb, and
young Crummell vowed to himself to one day become
a renowned scholar in America. And this he did. Recalling   this   episode   sixty–seven   years   later,
Crummell related the "crude asininity" of John C.
Calhoun   and   mockingly   observed,   "Mr.   Calhoun
expected the Greek syntax to grow in *Negro brains*,
by   spontaneous   generation."[41]   Crummell   felt   the
need to "prove" himself in America; however, as he
later   admitted,   he   had   never   lost   his   childhood
resolve to go to Africa.[42]

    As a twenty–one–year–old man, Crummell tried
to resolve this dilemma of having to choose either
Africa   or   America   by   proposing   a   philosophical
framework that would emphasize the principle of
unity. But he was transcending the problem on a
metaphysical plane and leaving the existential problem untouched. As a middle–aged man in his forties,
Crummell was still struggling to resolve the dilemma.
Living in Africa and seeking to recruit Afro–Americans to join him in his efforts to build a strong Liberian nation, he wrote in a letter to his American
brethren: "I am not putting in a plea for colonization."[43] But a few pages later on he asserted: "It is
the duty of black men to feel and labor for the salvation of the mighty millions of their kin all through

[their] continent [Africa]."⁴⁴ And he appealed openly: "Come over and help us."⁴⁵ Painfully, Crummell sought a compromise. Ultimately, it was in the way he lived his life that Crummell resolved this dilemma. For the present, this pulling at his heart and intellect from opposite sides of the Atlantic served as a motivating factor in his formulation of a Pan-African ideal.

Crummell observed that people like his father and Peter Williams were abandoning the idea of a literal unification between black Americans and Africans in favor of unity among black people in America. The ACS was actually promoting a separation between free Blacks and enslaved Blacks, and *Freedom's Journal* was one trumpet call to all black Americans to stand shoulder to shoulder and confront those who would enslave black people. The freedom of all black people must take priority over the return of some black people to their homeland. Crummell was inevitably caught up in this line of reasoning, and Pan-Africanism, at this stage of his development, meant black solidarity among American Blacks as *Freedom's Journal* had demonstrated.

As an eleven-year-old boy, Crummell witnessed another striking example of black solidarity on an organizational level—the establishment in 1830 of the National Convention of Colored People. Prompted, no doubt, by the expulsion of free black citizens from Cincinnati in 1829, black people organized themselves politically on a national level, and, for the first time, set about creating a black American political consciousness. During the first half of the nineteenth century, there were eight such national conventions (the inaugural and seven other conventions).⁴⁶

At these conventions, black leaders vigorously opposed the ACS and its African colonization schemes and stoutly defended their rights as American citizens. "The conduct of this institution [ACS] is

the most unprincipled that has been realized in almost any civilized county," they complained, and, on another occasion, with William Lloyd Garrison and Arthur Tappan* as observers, the convention resoundingly condemned the ACS for "pursuing the direct road to perpetuate slavery." On the question of colonization, they denounced any scheme to have free black Americans deported to Africa, though the 1833 convention was willing to countenance "voluntary emigration." Canadian settlements were encouraged for black citizens who were expelled from Cincinnati; however, this support for Canadian emigration was not to be construed as a possible alternative to citizenship rights: "In contributing to our brethren [in Canada] . . . we would not wish to be understood, as possessing inclination to remove . . . we rejoice in exclaiming—
    This is *Our* own,
    Our native land" (Emphasis in the original).
    Convention after convention reiterated the rights of black Americans and their duty "to adhere to the Declaration of Independence and the Constitution of the United States." The 1834 and 1835 conventions directed the delegates to return to their respective states and petition "to be admitted to the rights and privileges of American citizens." To buttress their struggle for civil rights, it was formally adopted at the 1835 convention that black Americans drop the words "colored" or "African" in describing themselves or their institutions.
    What particularly contributed to Crummell's development, however, was the Pan–Africanist appeal

---

*Both men initially had supported the ACS. They later "saw the light," and, at the 1832 Convention, Garrison debated the Reverend R. R. Gurley, secretary of the ACS, on the question of black deportation versus African colonization.

and deep interest in education that the conventions supported. Even while voicing negative sentiments about African colonization, the conventions proudly claimed that black Americans were descendants of Egyptians, and the African past was extolled as "an ancestry . . . whose glittering monuments stood forth as beacons, disseminating light and knowledge to the uttermost parts of the earth." Also, the conventions enthusiastically welcomed West Indians into their midst: a Reverend Mr. Harrison from Antigua was present at the 1832 convention, and a Mr. Evan Williams from Port-au-Prince, Haiti, attended the 1834 convention and was formally accepted as an honorary member. At the opening address of the 1831 convention, a Pan-African note was struck: "Our attention has been called to investigate the political standing of our brethren *wherever dispersed*" (my emphasis). Four years later, the 1835 convention voted to "open correspondence with gentlemen in Liberia." This concern for the condition of black people wherever they might be living anticipated Marcus Garvey's appeal to "Africans at home and abroad."

But education was an even more persistent concern at these conventions than the Pan-African appeal. In speeches, papers, resolutions, and committee reports, recommendations were made for the establishment of a manual labor school in which black "sons of the present and future generation may obtain a classical education and the mechanic arts in general." At the 1832 convention, Boston Crummell was on an education committee which Peter Williams, Jr., chaired; the following year, the convention body appointed William Lloyd Garrison to go to England to raise funds for building a school, and warmly applauded Miss Prudence Crandall's effort to establish a high school for colored females in Canterbury, Connecticut. Like his father, Crummell took an active part in the educational concerns of a later national convention.

After the 1835 convention, there was a deliberate break in the meetings of the national convention to allow delegates to organize state conventions to implement the resolutions taken at the national conventions. In 1840, a call went out for a New York State convention at which Crummell delivered the keynote address. The call stated explicitly that the primary objective of the convention was "to obtain a relief from those political disabilities under which we labor." The particular "political disability" was the Act of 1821 which required black citizens of New York to possess at least $250 in property to vote. In his address, Crummell argued this political question on grounds of birthright ("we are the descendants of some of the earliest settlers of the State") and service to the country ("The splendid naval achievements on Lake Erie and Champlain [during the War of 1812] were owing mostly to the skill and prowess of colored men."). But transcending both these arguments, Crummell rested his case on a higher right: "On the ground of our common humanity, do we claim equal and entire rights with the rest of our fellow citizens." Having publicly joined in the struggle for civil rights, Crummell made it unmistakably clear that the Declaration of Independence and the Constitution applied to black Americans: *"We are Americans.* We were born in no foreign clime . . . we profess to be American and republican, . . . [and] we should never have been deprived of an equal suffrage."[47] Though Crummell made no direct Pan-African appeal in this address, the display of black camaraderie and black unity in facing problems common to the race manifested the spirit of Pan-African unity.

In an effort to maintain this spirit of oneness, at the 1847 National Negro Convention, Crummell played the role of peacemaker between Garnet and Douglass[48] who had split over the question of the best means for achieving the abolition of slavery.

At the previous convention, from which Crummell was absent, Garnet had suggested that the enslaved black people should "take" their freedom "regardless of consequences" if slaveowners stubbornly resisted emancipation; Douglass persuaded the assembly against this approach. At the 1847 convention, Crummell worked with Douglass to prepare a paper acceptable to Garnet which recommended "moral suasion" as the way to rid the nation of slavery. Crummell emerged from this convention as the levelheaded black leader who prevented a split between the black leadership.

A thorough educational training and a notorious incident with Bishop Onderdonk had fitted Crummell for the grave responsibility of black leader at a national convention. After the Reverend Peter Williams's school, Crummell attended African Free School No. 2 on Mulberry Street which was run by Quakers under the direction of Charles Andrews.[49] The African Free Schools were established by the New York Manumission Society, a society that had been organized in New York in 1785 with John Jay as president and Alexander Hamilton as secretary. The aim of the Manumission Society was to organize the fight against slavery. In 1787, two years after it was founded, the Society established a free school "for the education of such persons as have been liberated from bondage."[50] The first free school grew and expanded until there were seven free schools, but in 1834, all seven schools were absorbed into the New York public school system.[51] According to Mr. Charles Andrews, the purpose of educating these free black children was "to fit them for the enjoyment and right understanding of their future privileges, and relative duties, when they should become free men and citizens."[52] The school thrived and more than satisfied its stated goal. There were regular "open house" invitations to the general public. Mr. Andrews recorded the exemplary performance of African Free

School students at an 1832 exhibition[53] and the stunning impression made by one of the pupils (Isaiah DeGrasse) whose navigation chart was exhibited to the American Convention in Baltimore in 1828.[54] In 1824, the Marquis de La Fayette (who had recruited Henri Christophe among the black Haitian troops who fought in the American War of Independence) visited New York and took time off from his official meetings to visit the Free School, and again the students performed brilliantly in a public examination.[55] In fact, so confident was Mr. Andrews in the preparation and training of African Free School students that in 1826 he threw out an open challenge to pit his students in a public examination against any students on a similar level from any New York school.[56] Actually, several black students did carry all the prizes of a collegiate academy in New York, but the prevailing response seemed to be "'Cui bono?' Will we feel any better to have waiters who read Virgil and Horace?"[57] Mr. Andrews was proud of the African Free Schools and their students.

χ When Crummell attended the African Free School, he made friends who strengthened his pride and faith in the ability of black people. His school-mates included the fierce agitator and outstanding orator, Henry Highland Garnet; the outstanding black physician, James McCune Smith; the saintly scholar and wit, Thomas S. Sidney; the great actor, Ira Aldridge; the brilliant orator and ablest thinker on his legs, Samuel Ringgold Ward; and others of that brilliant galaxy of young black minds that emerged in the early decades of the nineteenth century.

While he was a student at the African Free School, the Lancastrian or Monitorial Educational System was functioning. This system emphasized parent participation, rigid discipline, regular inspection, and oral work. The curriculum was rigorous and included astronomy, geography, grammar, spelling, reading, arithmetic, elocution, and penmanship.[58]

Crummell also learned from the African Free School
the system of using fellow students to be monitors of
groups of other students. This system encouraged
group effort and service. Instead of fierce competi-
tion to establish who was the brightest, the Lancastrian system encouraged cooperative effort in
which the one who first grasped a concept had as
monitor to teach this concept to his classmates. This
fostering of unified effort was especially important
for young scholars like Crummell who had to go out
and serve their less fortunate brethren. Crummell's
adult life was an extension of this teacher–service
role which a monitor served in the Lancastrian system. Under first the spiritual guidance of the Reverend Mr. Williams's school and next the God–fearing
instruction of the Quakers, Crummell was protected
from the hostile society of the white world. Thus, he
was encouraged to further his education.

However, for a free Black in the North during the
first half of the nineteenth century, getting an education beyond the elementary level often meant
risking one's life and enduring callous humiliation.
Miss Prudence Crandall was one of the white school
ma'ams (she would have been called "nigger lover" in
the South) who risked and was willing to sacrifice her
life, reputation, and career in order to help educate
black youth. Her case is a celebrated one. In 1831,
her house was surrounded by night riders, her win-
dows were broken, and she was dragged out of her
house, brought to trial, found guilty and imprisoned.
Her crime was opening a school for colored girls in
Canterbury, Connecticut. Though she subsequently
won the case on an appeal, she was held *persona non
grata* by most of the white community. This did not
stop Miss Crandall, however. At the second National
Negro Convention (1832) mention was made of Miss
Prudence Crandall's new high school for colored
females. Miss Crandall eventually had to leave Connecticut. Nor was this an isolated case. A black stu-

dent was known to attend Yale University, but he was made to sit in the corridor. In fact, up to 1833, under the laws in many northern states, any black person who attended a white institution was liable to receive no less than ten lashes on his or her naked back in public.[59] Crummell experienced some of the hostility meted out against black youths seeking an education beyond the secondary level, but he was not easily daunted. He had lived in times when the great Nat Turner challenged, in the name of God, the wickedness of slavery. As a young boy, he had actually witnessed "several refugees [after the Nat Turner insurrection] from South Langston County, Virginia, landing in New York in an open boat."[60] Crummell had known and seen the courage of black men.

Thus, when in 1835 the abolitionists of New Hampshire, under the leadership of the Reverend William Scales, opened the doors of Noyes Academy in Canaan to colored students, Crummell, together with his friends Garnet and Sidney, decided to attend. The journey from New York to New Hampshire exposed the sixteen–year–old Crummell to a personal experience of the harshness of life for a black person in America. The first leg of the journey was by steamboat from New York to Providence. These three young boys, well–dressed, polite and on their way to school, were permitted "no cabins, no beds, no food." They were exposed to the cold and the storm.[61] The second leg of the journey, roughly four hundred miles, was even worse. They had to travel on the top of the coach, changing at Boston, Concord, and Hanover.[62] These young ambitious boys were greeted with cold stares, jeers, and shameless insults. Crummell described the journey in his characteristic selfless manner: "Sidney and myself were his [Garnet's]companions during the whole journey; and I can never forget his sufferings—sufferings from pain and exposure, sufferings from thirst and hunger, sufferings from taunt and insult at every village and town, and oft times at every farmhouse. ... It seems hardly conceivable that Christian people could thus treat human beings travelling through a land of ministers and churches."[63] A cold coming they had of it! But the hostility intensified even more once they got there. They were invited by friends of Human Freedom at Plymouth in New Hampshire to participate in the July 4, Independence Day celebrations, and they all spoke at this gathering. We must note that even as younger boys, Crummell and a group of friends with Garnet as their leader had vowed that they would always commemorate July 4 with sackcloth and ashes until their enslaved brethren were emancipated. The first National Negro Convention (1831) had also adopted this policy of "humiliation, fasting and prayer" on July 4. Thus, when they spoke to this Independence Day gathering in New Hampshire, they were forthright rather than political. Crummell recounted Sidney's speech as being brilliant and impressive: "In severe and pointed terms did he dissect the hypocrisy of American Christianity and Republicanism."[64] Forthwith, the farmers from the surrounding area resolved that the academy was a public nuisance and had to be removed. A month following this resolution, these New Hampshire citizens seized the school building, and with ninety yoke of oxen dragged it into a nearby swamp. As Crummell contemptuously stated: "They were two days in accomplishing their miserable work."[65] Having destroyed the schoolhouse, the lynch mob in this North American Canaan next set upon the students. Garnet, who had a crippled leg which kept him in constant pain, organized the defense against these bullies. When the barn to which the students had fled was fired upon, Garnet responded with a discharge from a double-barreled shotgun, and "the coward ruffians did not stay." The students were able to return to New York in peace. Crummell had learned the importance of courage and physical force in defending one's life, and though he did not himself ever have recourse to the gun, he did display that moral daring that few men have the courage to sustain.

✗ Crummell was still determined to pursue a high school education. In the 1830s, there were only three high schools open to black youth in North America: Gettysburg, which Daniel Payne attended; Oberlin; and Oneida Institute, over which Beriah Green, that exemplary white philanthropist, presided. Crummell attended Oneida Institute, where he distinguished himself as a student.[66] Situated in Whitesboro, a village in Oneida County, New York, this school encouraged rigorous thinking.[67] While a student at Oneida Institute, Crummell concentrated on a very severe curriculum which included Greek and Roman history, English history, major English poets like Milton, Shakespeare, Coleridge, and Wordsworth, the classical languages—Latin, Greek, and Hebrew—the modern languages—German, and French—philosophy, and science. This heavy classical training in history and language and the romantic influence in poetry found their way into Crummell's thought and life. His Pan-African idealism bespoke the romantic idealism that suffused the work of Wordsworth, and the rigid, disciplined, and spiritual character that identifies Crummell was, in part, the fruit of his classical training. In addition to the demanding studies of his curriculum, Crummell had to face financial problems. While he was attending Oneida, his father apparently suffered financial reverses,[68] for young Crummell was soon left with very little to continue his education. As if not sufficiently restrained by his studies and his financial setbacks, Crummell chose to live a spartan existence while he studied at the institute. He shared a room opposite to Sidney's, and he recalled the almost medieval, hairshirt, saintly regimen that they imposed on themselves. They would get up very early in the morning and visit each other's room to study, and often Crummell said he found Sidney "in the dark, not unfrequently undressed, sometimes the room cold—in deep and fervent prayer."[69] Doubtless Crummell shared this kind of existence that went beyond self-sacrifice. Outside their academic work, these two young men conversed deeply and almost daily on scriptural doctrine, "often reading and studying the scared oracles in the original."[70]

At Oneida Institute, Crummell became settled in his mind to become a priest. The influence of Peter Williams, Jr., and a sermon by Bishop William Whittingham which Crummell claimed first made him think seriously of the priesthood[71] undoubtedly played a part in pointing him in the direction of the church. But the lofty pleasures he experienced from intense religious study and the physical life of asceticism which he entered into while a student at Oneida finally convinced him to pursue a religious vocation.

It could not have been an easy decision for Crummell to choose to become an Episcopal priest. He knew the racial prejudices and humiliation his mentor, Peter Williams, Jr., had to endure. Furthermore, while he was at Oneida, Garnet had relayed to him the hostile racist treatment DeGrasse had to endure by being "stuck up in a corner to eat" while a student at the General Theological Seminary. In the same letter, Garnet deplored the mistreatment suffered by George Moore, one of their African Free School peers.[72] Yet Crummell remained firm in the almost medieval piety he shared with Sidney and decided on a life of prayer and service. When he graduated from Oneida Institute in 1837,[73] he was ready for the rigorous trials that awaited him.

When Crummell returned to New York, Peter Williams, Jr., encouraged him to apply for entry into the General Theological Seminary. In his letter of resignation from the Antislavery Society, Williams had written, "It was exclusively our duty to labor to qualify our people for the enjoyment of [our] rights." Williams knew that black people would have to produce their own teachers and ministers if they were ever to be properly trained, and so he encouraged both Isaiah DeGrasse and Crummell to get formal theological training. DeGrasse had no visible traces of African blood, and he was at first admitted to the General Theological Seminary; however, when it was found out that he did have an "ascertainable drop of black blood," he was forced out of the seminary by Bishop Onderdonk. One year later (1838), Alexander Crummell, a perfectly black man of pure African descent, approached the very same Bishop Onderdonk seeking entrance into the General Theological Seminary. Crummell's application for admission to the seminary was intended to be a direct confrontation with this Christian institution. He had all the required qualifications, and the dean of the faculty, Dr. William Whittingham, who later became Crummell's bishop in Washington, D.C., was willing to accept him: "I would but it is out of my hands."[74] Bishop Onderdonk tried to persuade Crummell to withdraw his application, but on the advice of Williams, Crummell drew up a petition to the trustees of the seminary. This angered the bishop. The following day Crummell visited Onderdonk in his study, and as Crummell reported forty years later: "He [Onderdonk] set upon me with a violence and grossness that I have never since encountered, save in one instance, in Africa."[75] Bishop Onderdonk, who was head of the New York diocese, persuaded a general assembly of Christian ministers who were then meeting in New York to pass a law prohibiting black people from becoming part of their ministerial congregation. The next day, the bishop denied Crummell admission. Years later, this bishop was removed in disgrace from his bishopric due to his conduct in matters not related to race.

Crummell's rejection by the General Theological Seminary became a *cause célèbre* both inside and outside the black community. The leading black newspaper of the period, the *Colored American*, edited by Charles B. Ray, carried the story of Crummell's denial of admission to the seminary.[76] Crummell apparently attended an institution in Camden, New Jersey, after this rejection, for among his papers there is a letter from a fellow student which showed Crummell to be very active despite his recent setback.[77] Meanwhile, sentiments regarding the General Theological Seminary incident still simmered. In 1838, students at Oneida Institute published in the *Colored American* a resolution sympathetic to Crummell and condemning the actions of the General Theological Seminary.[78] One month later to the very day, Crummell was appointed agent for the New York *Colored American*.[79] Two months later we find Crummell opening up the whole issue of his denial of candidacy in the General Theological Seminary by publicly relating in the pages of the *Colored American* the difficulties black people face in getting into theological seminaries. Crummell gave in rather lengthy detail his encounter with Bishop Onderdonk and all the events leading to the final refusal of his admission to the seminary.[80] In order to clear up the claims by Bishop Onderdonk that Crummell sought his own dismissal, Crummell promised to publish in the *Colored American* the correspondence he exchanged with the bishop. John Jay wrote to Crummell offering to insert a paragraph in the *Colored American* to the effect that "Bishop Onderdonk did not dismiss you *at your own request*." John Jay urged Crummell not to publish the correspondence and to let him have the letters. As a postscript to the letter, Jay informed Crummell that he had a donation of twenty dollars from Gerrit

Smith and requested: "Say to whom to pay it."[81] Crummell never published the correspondence, but John Jay's paragraph never appeared in the *Colored American*. There is no evidence that the "postscript" offer was ever taken up. For many years, Crummell's name was always linked with the General Theological Seminary's discriminatory practices against black people. However, the General Theological Seminary experience did not deter Crummell, and on the advice of well-meaning white friends, he went to Boston where Bishop Alexander V. Griswold welcomed him, and in 1840 he became a candidate for orders. On May 30, 1842, Crummell was ordained to the diaconate, in St. Paul's Church, Boston, and, in December 1844, he was ordained to the priesthood by the Right Reverend Alfred Lee in Philadelphia.[82]

One would have thought that after the experiences of Canaan, New Hampshire, and the insults and humiliation of Bishop Onderdonk, Crummell had completed the ordeal of his Herculean Labors. But this was not to be. He was a marked man, and there was universal anger against him. First, he tried to get a parish in Providence, Rhode Island, but had no support. Next, he tried Philadelphia and was told that he would be received on condition that he never applied for a seat at the convention of the Episcopal Church. Crummell promptly responded, "That . . . I shall never do."[83] He tried Boston but to no avail. Finally, he went to his home city, New York. Here, too, Crummell found no support. Without the support of the whole body of the church, Crummell found it difficult to get started. For a short time, he was a schoolteacher for colored children in New York, but it was the ministry, for which he was trained, that he settled into. He labored hard, but, according to his account, were it not for the assistance from white philanthropists like Dr. Stephen H. Tyng, rector of St. George's Church, and his patron John Jay, he might have died from starvation. "I have suffered persecution, injury, poverty, hunger, almost nakedness,"[84] Crummell wrote. He became seriously ill, and, indeed, it was not until he lived in Africa that he fully recovered. While he labored almost fruitlessly in New York City, friends advised him to go to England to raise money to build his own church. He acceded to the advice, and in January 1848, he sailed for England.

The final years of the decade of the thirties had been a bleak and dismal time for Crummell. In 1835, he was almost lynched in Canaan; in 1836–1837, his father's business had collapsed, and DeGrasse was humiliated, then dismissed from the General Theological Seminary; between 1838 and 1840, he lost his two dear sisters, and on June 17, 1840, his very close friend, Thomas Sidney, died. In a letter to a friend expressing grief over Sidney's death, Crummell wrote, "The loss of such a friend completely unmans me," and though Crummell yielded humbly, "My Lord, thy will be done," he could not quiet the hurt and admitted to himself, "My wicked heart rebels." The cumulative effect of his misfortunes was weighing heavily on Crummell, but instead of relief, further disaster struck. A few months after Sidney's death, his mentor and spiritual advisor, the Reverend Peter Williams, Jr., died. Crummell was a poor man, and in 1841, he did not have enough money to go to Providence, Rhode Island. There is a note among his personal papers about one Thomas M. Clark sending him part of the passage (fifteen dollars) and suggesting other people who might help.[85] Poverty, want, and sickness were afflicting Crummell's body and soul. Virulent Negro hatred ran high in church and state alike. When Chief Justice Taney later ruled in 1857, "The Negro has no right which white men were bound to respect," he was expressing quite accurately the sentiments of the nation in the decade of the forties. During these trying times, Crummell might have thought of Africa as a more promising prospect, but escape from persecution would not be his driving motivation. At the 1840 New York State Convention, Crummell would defy the Taneys and the colonization societies, and he would exclaim loudly on behalf of all black people, "We are Americans."

EMERGING THOUGHT OF CRUMMELL

Before he left for England, however, Crummell made his mark as a scholar and an orator in black America. It is to his early writings that we now turn. Crummell's extant writings during the first phase of his life (1819–1847)[86] touched on three basic themes—politics, religion, and education. These three themes interlocked so closely that they, in effect, established a framework of philosophical thought which deepened rather than changed during Crummell's lifetime. His first noteworthy literary effort was his "Eulogy on the Life and Character of Thomas Simpkins Sidney,"[87] which was delivered before the Phoenixonian Literary Society of the city of New York, on July 4, 1840. As was noted above, Crummell and Sidney were very close friends who were classmates at the African Free School, shared the Canaan experience together, and studied together at Oneida Institute. However, Sidney died at the age of twenty–three before he had a chance to fulfill the promise he had shown as a young man, and Crummell had the sad duty of eulogizing his close friend. Beyond its lamentation, in this eulogy can be traced the lines which undergirded Crummell's basic philosophical system of thought. There was really nothing new or original in Crummell's thoughts. Both Otey Scruggs, who has written best on Crummell, and Wilson Moses, in his *Golden Age of Black Nationalism,* correctly observed that Crummell's general ideas reflected nineteenth–century Victorian thought. The significant fact is that he put his personal stamp of approval on these ideas and modified them to suit his Pan–African goals. He made these Victorian ideas and values his own and expressed them in his own terms and through his own experience.

Early in the eulogy, Crummell defined his structure of the human psyche: "The love we have for the manifestation of power is not the off–spring of either instinct or passion; but one of the plainest and spontaneous exercises of Reason" (S3). He clearly distinguished between instinct, passion, and reason, and in Platonic fashion, he placed reason above the other two. He cherished reason as being the highest faculty of the human psyche, and he did not challenge the human love for the manifestation of power as being a negative urge which ought to be suppressed. Reason, he went on to say, was "an universal and native sentiment," sentiment being used in the sense of a deep–felt knowledge, a kind of reflexive recognition of truth—hence, "spontaneous." This reflexive recognition of truth was an ability with which all men were born ("universal and native"), instinct and passion being peculiar to each individual in that they both issued from the external environment. Reason, emanating from within, was a faculty *in*–formed in man. Man was infused with Absolute Truth, and his recognition of this information was common to all men and so, according to Crummell, "attests divine origin." Spontaneous or reflexive reason was intuition that came to man as being self–evident or axiomatic.

But not all reason was spontaneous. There was another level of reason that came to man as a result of efforts exerted. Sometimes intuitive perception came as a result of the exertion of "intellectual and moral powers." It was true that speaking about Sidney, Crummell stated, "With him the perception of Truth was intuitive" without struggles like other men. This suggested a kind of *spontaneous reason*. But this intuitive understanding of Sidney's was not pure reflex action. We must remember that this kind of spontaneity came about because of his intense intellectual effort ("constant intellectual exercise" [S20] and "unceasing thought and continual investigation" [S21]), and his powerful religious drive ("I found him in the dark, not unfrequently undressed, sometimes the room cold—in deep and fervent prayer" [S28]). Though the intuitive insight comes in a flash, it does not just happen! Intuition is the result of earnest and constant effort in both the intellectual *and* moral spheres. For Crummell, education readied the intellectual powers and religion honed the moral powers. These two concerns, therefore, would dominate all of Crummell's life. But his educational and religious programs would have always as their objectives the sharpening of the intellectual and moral powers within man, with the aim of allowing him to perceive intuitively "those awful truths, those eternal principles" (S4).

Of grave importance is Crummell's meaning of the term "eternal principles." By the use of the appositive instead of the coordinate structure in his phrase "those awful truths, those eternal principles" (*not* "those awful truths *and* those eternal principles"), it is clear that Crummell intended "truths" and "principles" to be understood as synonyms. Like Pilate, then, we must ask that eternal question: What is Truth? Crummell approached the answer obliquely: "Truth is always a hidden and unsightly existence . . . to those whose mental vision has been blurred." In other words, Truth was what the mental vision perceived. But what was this mental vision? There were two hints to this answer in the Sidney eulogy. First, it was faith, and, second, it was the moral sensibilities. Referring again to the "hidden and unsightly existence," Crummell wrote that there were "unseen but living realities of spiritual existence" which only faith could penetrate (S33–S34). There seemed to be in Crummell's cosmology, a world outside our sensual world, a world unreachable through our sensual faculties, a world that remained untouched by empirical reasoning. This was why Crummell divided philosophy into two broad areas, Sensual Philosophy and Spiritual Philosophy. The former probed the world of the senses, but it was Spiritual Philosophy that delved into this world outside our sensual world, into the "living realities of spiritual existence." This is the world of Truth, the world of fundamental principles. This world could be entered into or reached through *faith*. By itself, this explanation does not take us very far; however, there is a fortunate circumstance in Crummell's manuscript where, apparently for stylistic purposes, he replaced the phrase "mental vision," which he had used in the sentence before, with the phrase "moral sensibilities." Obviously, he thought the phrases interchangeable. Even as we had faculties that allowed us to perceive and know the sensual world, so did we have faculties through which we could apprehend the spiritual world. The faculties that allowed us to apprehend the spiritual world were our moral sensibilities. It was an innate intelligence on which we must rely, therefore, in order to grasp these hidden principles or laws. Ultimately, it was a kind of intuitive belief, faith, that led us into this world beyond our world. Our moral sensibilities issued from faith. Crummell was not here using faith in the strict theological sense, but in the sense of an intu- itive intelligence, in the sense of a mental vision as opposed to a sensual vision. This kind of faith is belief in something one *does* see, but since what one sees is not of the sensual world, the vision is not with the eyes. The spiritual world can be perceived only through the mind. It is important for us to realize that for Crummell this spiritual world was real, as real as the sensual world, a world, as he calls it, of "living realities." He was not a mere twenty–one– year–old youngster playing with words, for even as a seventy–seven–year–old man who had lived on three different continents, he was still aware of this world beyond our world: "It is an awful but also a majestic truth that even while we are in the flesh, and moving about amid earthly relations, we are already in the invisible world."[88]

Crummell's philosophical posture was evidently in the Platonic rather than Aristotelian tradition, or, within the theological sphere, he followed the pathway of his African ancestor, St. Augustine, rather than that of St. Thomas Aquinas. The phenomenal world of the senses, "this dim spot men call Earth," was, for Crummell, accidental not substantial. Crummell's thought, however, was not strictly Platonic, for he did not dismiss our world of the senses as a mere shadow, a mere imitation of the Ideal World; rather, he saw our world as an incomplete manifestation of the real world. Our world was accidental in the sense that it was more potentiality than actuality; our world possessed the seeds of substance and had to be seen as such. For Crummell, there was a more organic than mechanical relationship between the phenomenal world and the world beyond it. Indeed, our world was not so much false ("a shadow") as it was incomplete, and it was man's duty and responsibility to help complete this imperfect world. It was a dynamic world of becoming that Crummell perceived, not a static world of being, a world defined and fixed by its imitative character. Human nature, therefore, was seen as "the image of God," capable of forever approaching though never reaching its goal. Much like Sir Thomas Browne, Crummell felt that if our spiritual consciousness were properly developed, "We might admire the mysterious framework of our own being, and stand in wonder and admiration before the inconceivable greatness and majesty of the eternal mind" (S18). The key words were "wonder" and "admire." He used "wonder," not in the modern verbal sense of doubtful questioning ("I wonder if he is coming"), but in the nominal sense of "awe." We stand in awe at the majesty of God. So, too, "admi-

ration" was not used in the modern passive sense of
feeling approval for a thing or person, feeling joy
over ("I admire his singing"), but in the active sense
as the Latin roots of the word suggest, *admirare*—to
look at, or more precisely, to look toward, for "ad"
has the force of "motion toward." There must be an
active looking at; the admirer has to participate in
the object being admired; he has judiciously to
scrutinize the object. A judicious, a carefully
balanced admiration of the phenomenal world would
help us to recognize God's hand in His creation and so
allow us to see Truth, to see the fundamental
principles operating. Very crucial and central to
Crummell's thought was that mere contemplation
would not suffice in our performing our duty of
completing the world. Always Crummell insisted on
the practical aspect of applying the fundamental
principles to "our sad spot which we call Earth." He
quotes Milton on this matter, "to learn and know and
thence to do" (S8). When, therefore, he defined
religion, he saw it as thought *and conduct* (S30).
Indeed, he praised Sidney because he (Sidney)
grounded his politics on the Bible. The Holy Word was
not merely for contemplation; it had to become the
framework for action. Certainly, contemplation and
reverence were due, not as ends in themselves but to
aid us in reaching those fundamental laws, in discovering the unchanging Truths. Once we had grasped
some of these principles, they were to be "transformed into effective instruments, the active Agents
of Right and Holiness" (S19). The purpose of Spiritual
Philosophy was not to indulge in abstruse theorizing,
catching at shades and splitting hairs; rather, it was
to serve as part of the educational process which
exercised the moral sensibilities, thereby imparting
acuteness and perspicuity to our mental vision.
    A direct, practical bearing of this other world of
reality on our world was the question of slavery and
racial oppression. There were great political prin-

ciples or laws that had to be evinced and activated in
our world. One of these great principles was brotherhood, fraternity. The unalterable Truth was not an
individual pursuit of happiness, meaning by that,
personal indulgence and satisfaction of personal
desires; rather, happiness lay in the helping of others
in one's relentless pursuit of Truth. "How delightful,"
Crummell apostrophized, "how soul-searching . . . [to
find] a few men living not for themselves . . . but
giving up their existence to the cause of the Truth"
(S26). Thus, what distinguished Sidney in Crummell's
eyes, after that abominable experience he, Sidney,
and Garnet suffered in Canaan, was the fact that
Sidney reflected "not upon his own wrongs, but those
of his people . . . the . . . monstrous oppression which
have well nigh shrivelled our humanity" (S15). This, to
Crummell, was the fundamental principle of unity
being put into action by Sidney. The liberating of
black people and the dissecting of the "hypocrisy of
American Christianity and Republicanism was not the
unifying of merely black people, but the unifying of
the whole nation" (S14). Fighting for the liberation of
black people was a patriotic act. Indeed, working for
the enfranchisement of black people bespoke patriotic aspirations; more, it meant, finally, fighting the
cause of mankind. As long as there were oppressed
people, downtrodden people living in abject poverty,
the human family suffered. The law of unity inter-
connected the highest with the lowest, and one weak
link in the chain of being destroyed the chain. For
this larger reason, the cause of black people became
for Crummell "the sacred cause." It was not only a
sentimental, chauvinistic, self-survival cause that
Sidney advanced when he devoted his entire life to
the political elevation of his people; he was championing the cause of Truth.

   The important point here is not whether we agree
with Crummell's reasoning or not, but the fact that
as a mere twenty-one-year-old young man, he was

seeking and rationalizing a philosophical framework for right action. Even as he felt it was not sufficient for man to recognize that he had the good fortune, the opportunity, the privilege to gaze upon the wonders of God's creation, but he must acknowledge that it was his *duty* to contemplate God's grandeur, so he felt that self-survival and humanitarian urges were not enough in fighting for the liberation of black people, but man must realize that it was his *duty* to aid in the struggle. Black people, in particular, had to realize that it was their *duty*, not optional right, to commit their lives to the welfare of their people. So it was, in voicing the purpose of the Phoenixonian Society (which Sidney had founded), Crummell used the language of prayer and sacrifice, when like a priest he solemnly prayed: "[We] offer up the incense of our youthful hearts, on the strength and purposes of our more mature years, at the common Altar or our people's good. Whatever of Talent or Genius we might each of us possess . . . we [come] together and [lay] it down as offering . . . for the great purposes of a poor despised and oppressed people" (S1).[89] These words expressed more than concern for fellow black people; they had an almost incantatory effect of a vow, of some pledge by a religious acolyte seeking to liberate some Truth, some fundamental principle among mankind. Yes, it was unconstitutional to oppress the black man as he was being oppressed, but more, it was unprincipled, in the deepest sense of that word.

The first step in the black man's duty toward his race was racial unity—without it, how could he expect unity with the rest of the human family? Black people must be united in a fraternal bond if only as a symptomatic manifestation of that greater brotherhood which the law of unity demanded. There was a tinge of impatience in Crummell's tone as he appealed to the fellow members of the Phoenixonian Society: "Do not a common ancestry, and common wrongs and oppression bind us together? . . . Should we not feel our hearts binding us together in bonds of brotherhood?" (S46). However, though a black man should suffer no one to tread upon him, at the same time, he should never consider himself better than common humanity. Thus, this unity of black brotherhood would help defend the black man from ruthless exploiters, but never, never should a cult of racial superiority be allowed to rear its ugly head. Black unity is not racism in the modern sense of that word, but merely a stage toward the final grand rendezvous when all men shall be brothers. The law of unity, the great Truth demanded this.

And herein lies another characteristic of a fundamental principle: It inexorably works itself out. This world of ours, governed as it is by the other world of principles, is a deterministic world. Finally, Truth will prevail. Man's responsibility is to help work out this process, but the ultimate end is inevitable. By inserting himself in the process, man can either speed it up or slow it down, but never can he change it. Man has but to see, through his mental vision, what the fundamental principle is and then work with it. No matter what the obstacles and obstruction, the man with the vision of Truth ultimately conquers—even if posthumously. Very explicitly Crummell stated, "Fundamental principles ultimately will have to be acceded to" (S35), and referring to obstructionists of the Truth, he approvingly quoted Sidney, "They will have to come up to it [Truth]" (S36). This explained why once one perceived a Truth, one had to follow where it led. Once under the spell of intuitive knowledge, one was led on by intuitive insights, not forcing intellectual judgments on these truths: "Where it [intuitively perceived truth] led there he [Sidney] immediately took his position"(S33).

But who perceives the Truth? Who has the mental vision? Who has the faith? In other words, who are the leaders? Here was where Crummell gave us the first glimmerings of the much later theory of the Talented Tenth: "The race not infrequently has been blessed with a superior class of men, whose intense desire has been to be controlled by Principle as the habit of the soul—to go through the world unmindful of the inclinations of sense and passion, with cheerful godliness, submitting to the dictates of Reason, working continually for the glory of God and the spiritualization of man "(S32). Two important facts can be gleaned from this statement. First, and perhaps the more important is that Crummell believed in a superior class of people. The second fact is that Crummell believed that the superior people were characterized by their intense desire to live lives controlled by "Principle." Taken out of the context of the entire eulogy, one would be inclined to describe Crummell as an elitist (in the worst sense of that word), and then callously concede that he had what was coming to him from white racists who were merely elitists of race. But this is unfair. As was pointed out above, Crummell argued that no man should separate himself from common humanity. On the other hand, one has to admit that his Talented Tenth statement does smack of the "innercircle mentality," and this is not inconsistent with Crummell's deterministic philosophy. The phenomenal world was incomplete, and the other world provided the laws, the principles, the truths that would work towards the completion of this world. It seemed logical that great spiritual leaders who had the mental vision to see these principles would have to come forward. It was a theory dangerously close to the doctrine of the Divine Elect, and Crummell was walking a tightrope between the chosen few and common humanity. But he walked well and never faltered because of the definition he gave to the superior class of people. The superior class was composed of people given to the spiritualization of man; they were people whose energies were directed toward serving others not themselves, and all for the greater glory of God. Men who were guided by reason, spontaneous or labored, could belong to this superior class. Let anyone who was willing to lay down his life for his brethren come forth; he belonged to this superior class. Crummell's Talented Tenth was not composed of people who had superior privilege and education, but people who were willing to endure superior sacrifice for others. One almost feared to be a member of Crummell's Talented Tenth, so awesome the responsibilities, so demanding the duties. When toward the end of his life Crummell did establish the American Negro Academy, his fundamental aim was still the same. In the inaugural address, he reiterated his Talented Tenth philosophy: "Every man in a race cannot be a philosopher; nay, but *few men* in any land, in any age, can grasp ideal truth."[90] The operative phrase in this statement is "ideal truth." Crummell is still speaking about fundamental principles not mere academic learning. Pure academic scholars were not Crummell's idea of the superior class: "If the [academic scholars] are not inspired with the notion of leadership and *duty* [emphasis mine], then with all their Latin and Greek and science they are but pedants, trimmers, opportunists."[91] It was a dutiful service that the Talented Tenth must offer. There must be nothing of the puffed-up superiority or personal aggrandizement usually associated with leadership. For Crummell's superior class of men, "*disinterestedness* must animate their motives and their acts."[92] It is true that as a seventy-eight-year-old man he recognized the limitation of the masses even as he did as a twenty-one year old: "The masses, nowhere are, or can be, learned or scientific;"[93] but, in the same way, as a young man he pleaded for association with common humanity, so, as an elderly man he displayed belief in the masses when he urged the members of the academy to seek out "the latent genius, garnered up, in the by–places and sequestered corners of this neglected Race."[94] Talent and inclination defined Crummell's elitism, not privilege and class. In an eloquent passage, he stated his position: "Neither property, nor money, nor station, nor office, nor lineage, are fixed factors, in so large a thing as the destiny of man. . . . The greatness of peoples springs from their ability to grasp the grand conceptions of being. It is the absorption of a people, of a nation, or a race, in large majestic and abiding things which lifts them up to the skies."[95]

Crummell widened and deepened his thinking as he matured in life, especially in regard to the role of the masses, but his abiding faith in the first principles stayed with him. That mental vision which opened up the world and allowed us to get glimpses of the "abiding things" remained central to his life. When he eulogized Sidney, he already spoke as one who had glimpses of the real world: "The veil that intercepts our vision they [fundamental principles] remove and instantly open our straining eyes to visions of glory and splendor; and light—eternal light—bursts in from a thousand quarters" (S36). This was his Christian spiritual vision. Again, when he saw in Sidney, "great Truths emanat[ing] . . . as sparks from a Blacksmith's forge" (S19), Crummell displayed this spiritual gift to see beyond the phenomenal world. Indeed, he related to Sidney on a spiritual level. As an eleven–year–old boy, Crummell wrote, "I felt my soul grow toward him [Sidney]" (S7). This eulogy on Sidney was a kind of vow, a self-consecration to the purposes of Truth and self-dedication to live with an unswerving adherence to principle.

But the mental vision is not an unearned gift. Correct religious practice and proper education were the major ways to develop moral sensibilities. In the first phase of his life, Crummell did, on two occasions, speak and write, on what he considered to be "proper education." We must remember that the steadfast aim of any enterprise, for Crummell, had to be the development of mental vision or the spiritualization of man. With that in mind, let us examine Crummell's treatises on education.

In his first treatise on education, Crummell held steadfast to his belief that the proper goal of mankind is the pursuit of Truth.[96] Arguing in his a priori manner, as he was wont to do, he asserted that, in order that man might perform his human duty, God in His wisdom must have placed in each human being a faculty that would allow man to apprehend Truth. This faculty is the intellect. For Crummell, then, education was the development of the intellect in order to enable it to apprehend Truth. He entirely rejected knowledge for knowledge's sake, and he railed against intellects that become perverted by seeking cleverness and scepticism as ends in themselves: "We want no Voltaires nor Humes, no Diderots nor Gibbons among us" (E53). Indeed, so relentless was he in following through on his basic premise of education that he stated the ultimate, "Better slavery than a godless education" (E53). This dogmatic approach led to a narrowness of view which was perhaps the most serious limitation of Crummell. But this shortcoming was mitigated by the fact that Crummell was fully aware of the reality of a spiritual world contiguous to this world of the senses, and, in pursuing this spiritual reality, he brooked nothing that smacked of diversion. The reality of this "other world" impinged so forcefully on Crummell's consciousness that time and again he reiterated that man "is surrounded by a host of invisible spirits" (E30), but he noted that easy communication with these spirits was not possible because of the "infirmities of sense and flesh." It was necessary, therefore, to be uncompromising in the pursuit of this spiritual world.

Failure to improve and expand the intellect was tantamount to closing off an individual's development of self and to setting up a barrier to the advancement of truth and the prayers of man. Ignorance did not mean that man would merely be in a state of stagnation, rather it developed in man an understanding of wrong principles. Man was in a dynamic state of becoming, and, if he did not discover right principles, then he would be led by wrong principles. This was why Crummell saw African peoples as wandering in the misty mazes of superstition. On the spectrum of knowledge, these unenlightened Africans were opposite to the Humes and Voltaires, yet the one complemented the other. In both cases, right principles were being neglected. It was easier to understand Crummell's debunking of a Voltaire, for he saw the French sceptic as being more clever than wise. Indeed, he warned that education "must never exalt the intellect above the Moral Principle" (E56). However, in the case of the African, why did not Crummell think that he (the African) could get inner visions and understanding of the world of right principles without Christian doctrine? He might justly argue that Christ came to show man the way, but surely it was unreasonable to assume that before Christ and in nations without knowledge of Christ, men's intellects could not serve their proper use! In fact, in later years, Crummell would soften this inflexible position concerning the state of the uneducated African. For the present, however, he earnestly felt that education (that is, development of the intellect toward its proper use) was a responsibility and duty of mankind. To neglect education was to neglect the development of the intellect and so thwart the plan of God who must have had some end in view for man's intellect.

Crummell not only believed that each person possessed, at least in potential form, the faculty to allow him to perceive the invisible world of first principles, but also felt that this faculty could be developed. He stoutly defended the inalienable right of children to be given the opportunity "to make efforts in science and literature which usually are the privilege of but a favored few" (E59). Hopefully, by having their "spheres of acquaintance" encouraged, children would be able to perceive with clearer inner vision the right principles that govern our world. Adults, too, needed to realize that the true pursuit of happiness consisted not in sensual pleasure but in an educated intellect that could recognize how "the great principles appear in the relations to one another." Crummell could imagine nothing more repulsive than "an old man barren in mind burning with lustful passions, but burnt out!" (E20). The intellect never cloyed: "The objects of the intellect are unlimited" (E20), and so a proper education provided the highest form of happiness.

Much as Crummell saw education as the tool for sharpening the intellect in order that mankind might apprehend the reality of the invisible world, his frame of reference was always his black world: It was the black perspective on education that dominated Crummell's discourse. Crummell felt that black Americans, in particular, needed to commit themselves to a proper education. On the practical level, he pointed out that poor living conditions had fostered in black people "the humbler and gentler traits," and the development of the mind and a strong character had been neglected. A slavish spirit, born of ignorance, was not true humility, and it was education that would urge black people to aspire to the highest and noblest offices (E12). Black Americans would never enjoy full citizens' rights and privileges as long as they remained in "dependence" occupations, serving as mere instruments of labor rather than shapers of policy. It was imperative for black people to begin understanding the scientific aspects of agriculture and the operations of the mercantile systems (E15,16). Moreover, if black people wished to eradicate slavery and racial discrimination in America, they must throw off their mental inertness and cultivate their intellect. Crummell was not really placing the blame for the black man's condition solely on the shoulders of black people; he was merely acknowledging that if black people did not help themselves educationally by training thousands of teachers, they would forever remain in the soul-crushing system of servitude and caste (E17, 18, 19). In stirring language, he castigated black people for being too conscious of being black, and he proudly declared, "We must throw off the servile notions . . . [and] must rise to clearer conceptions of our manhood" (E28). Much later in life (1885) he would publicly clash with Frederick Douglass on this very issue. He would urge, then, that black people stop wallowing in their slave experiences and look forward to shaping their own future: "Indeed we do live in two worlds, . . . the past and . . . the future, [but] DUTY lies in the future."[97] Throughout his life, without ever exonerating the white race from its crimes against black people, Crummell saw it incumbent upon his black brothers to seek their own ennoblement of character. He would always insist that the great minds of the past must be studied if one wanted to be stamped with great thoughts: "Lofty minds . . . live loftily together" (E30).

However, as much as he saw education as helping to serve the practical need for the social and economic uplift of black people, Crummell remained steadfast in championing as the first and highest purpose of education the nurturing of the moral nature of man, be he black or white. He urged aspiring black intellectuals to seek out, not the academic grove, but "the sweet retreats of piety" (E52). Immoral leaders would mean unspeakable dangers, and so it was a Christian education that needed to be sought. Thus, the education the black man sought and acquired must be used to destroy slavery and caste, not for personal gain but "to serve truth and duty" (E18). The moral principle being served when racial bigotry and exploitation were struck fatal blows was the principle of human brotherhood. With double underscoring of each word for emphasis, Crummell claimed: "<u>This is the age of brotherhood and humanity</u>" (E62). It was more to serve this moral principle of mankind than to enjoy practical gains that he urged education for black people.

Three years after this 1844 testimonial on education before the Hamilton Lyceum, Crummell further expanded his views on education before the 1847 National Convention of Colored People.[98] To a large extent, Crummell repeated to the convention what he had said in the 1844 testimonial on the practical aspect of education, but he played down the importance of a religious education. His thinking was very progressive in that he recommended a holistic approach to the education of black people. He pointed out that man was a being of mind, body, and soul. He felt that, so far, the black man had developed his body ("a hardy race") and his spirit ("a religious people"), but "We are lacking intelligence, scholarship and science." As he did in his 1844 testimonial, he suggested that learning would wipe away the stigma of inferiority, and he urged classical austerity and not romantic self–indulgence. Discipline, he thought, would bring the mental development that black people lacked. Moreover, Crummell went beyond the practical benefits of education, and again emphasized the moral responsibility of black people to develop that faculty of intellect which would allow them to apprehend the invisible world of first principles. Though Crummell was very conscious of the black race in his report, he did recommend that all works of genius, be they English, Roman, German, or Greek be "skillfully appropriated for [our] advancement." The last phrase is important, for he is not recommending an indiscriminate ingestion of Western thought; rather, he is proposing that the works of Western scholars be strained and graded and finally refined so that they would work for the development of the black man. After observing the woeful state of education for the black man (two badly run high schools for four hundred thousand people, very few colleges opened to black students, the ill preparation of those black students who did get admitted to college and their subsequent high drop–out rate), Crummell made his most compelling and perceptive observation: "While at college [young black people] are separated from their people." The educated black youth had to leave behind what should be his very sustenance and *raison d'être*. The result, Crummell realized, would be a class of black people who should be leaders separated from the masses and from their own social foundation. Black education for Crummell was not the studying of black literature, but an education which made one feel responsible to one's black brothers. This is the "pull theory" which Du Bois, a protégé of Crummell's, would later recommend in his essay, "Of the Training of Black Men" in *The Souls of Black Folk*. Finally, Crummell came up with eleven resolutions, the most outstanding being "the founding of a college [along the manual labor plan]" primarily for colored youth "but which shall not be exclusive."

From this paper on education, we can see that the twenty–eight–year–old Crummell was committed to the development of the black man's intellect. Minister though he was, he realized that for the soul of man to grow to its fullest capacity, the mind too must be nurtured. Slavery in America was built on the systematic starving of the black man's mind. Not only was the slave deprived of formal education, but the free blacks who scraped and crawled their way through some course of intellectual training were ridiculed and hardly ever rewarded in the form of just employment. The rebuilding of this starved and submerged facet of the black man's psyche was young Crummell's greatest ambition. Not only for pragmatic considerations but also for higher spiritual enlightenment must education be given priority in the black man's development. Thus, throughout the 1847 convention report on education, we find the resolutions laced with phrases like "the culture of the intellect," "advancing civilization," "intellectual improvement," "erudition and learning," and so forth. Much later in his life, Crummell would establish an academy (1897) with much the same goals as he recommended in 1847. Fifty years of living intensely in America, England, and Africa would only confirm these early thoughts of Crummell's.

If education had to have as its primary purpose the preparing of man that he might properly perceive the realities, the first principles of the invisible world contiguous to our three–dimensional world, religion was defined by this spiritual end. In his many sermons which have survived in his handwriting, we can see Crummell repeatedly advocating the spiritual goal for which man must strive. Preaching on the "Law of Liberty" in 1840,[99] Crummell carefully pointed out that "by no means" did he disagree with those who sought political freedom, but he stressed and insisted that "true freedom depends on the spiritual condition" (15). Political freedom was necessary, not only for humanitarian reasons, but because it was consistent with the law of God. If man would submit to God's general law, he would get powerful for he was made to fit in with this law (8). In an 1843 sermon,[100] Crummell again pointed to the spiritual nature of man which needed to be developed. Appealing to his colored brethren he warned, "We are not spiritual enough" (9). By 1847, Crummell would modify this position somewhat when in the convention paper on education he argued that the black man had developed his body and spirit and now needed to develop his intelligence and scholarship. Of course, the political setting of a convention could have prompted his position for he consistently felt that the development of reason had to be accompanied by the development of the "spiritual eye" in man. In his 1840 sermon on liberty, he clearly stated that the law of God was the law of reason because "it [the law of reason] brings us into accordance with the infinite of the Universe" (7). However, the reason of which he spoke, we must remember, could sometimes be "spontaneous reason" or intuition, and in the 1843 sermon in which he claimed that his black brethren were not spiritual enough, he claimed that "fundamental principles" were perceived through "intuition." In another 1843 sermon, "The Existence and Essence of God," Crummell ended on a very mystical note: "Every object of animation in the earth speaketh of God. Oh listen to the voice of nature and of God now" (13). Certainly it was to the spiritual intelligence that Crummell was appealing when he pleaded to his audience "to listen to the voice . . . of God."[101] It is to no sensual ear that he referred but to the metaphysical ear. The metasound of nature was clear to all who have ears to hear, and the experience was intuitive. Time and time again throughout his sermons Crummell warned: "The earthmonger is enslaved."[102] However, though man's guide must be intuitive, yet he needed proper direction. Thus, in an 1845 sermon, "Thy Kingdom Come,"[103] after asserting that if Jesus reigned He would get rid of slavery, Crummell indicted Asia, Europe, and notably Africa which was given up to "heathenism, superstition and concubinage" (6). It was clearly Crummell's feeling that Africa needed Christian guidance if its intuitive native genius were ever to find proper expression. In the first half of the nineteenth century, Christianity was to Western civilization what technology is today. Thus, when Crummell urged Christianity on to Africa, he was being as narrow-minded and dogmatic as many of today's well-wishers who urge modern technology as Africa's redemption. The special concern that Crummell showed for Africa, his Pan-African strain breaking through, was further underscored in this same sermon when he appealed to the Christian church to send "hordes of well-trained teachers," as the Mohammedans had done, to pull Africa out of the throes of paganism. Christian doctrine and training offered the proper discipline needed to hone the intuitive reason of man so that it could better comprehend the eternal verities of the invisible world of principles. Africa was in dire need of Christian missionaries, and to Africa Crummell would go. But before Africa, England!

One more work of Crummell's, his most outstanding literary work, must be examined before we follow him across the Atlantic. On December 26, 1846 (ten months before his 1847 treatise on education before the National Convention), Crummell delivered a eulogy described by one scholar as the best "oratorical effort of any colored man in the antebellum days."[104] Entitled "Eulogium on the Life and Character of Thomas Clarkson, Esq. of England,"[105] this address was a landmark in the development of a black prose style in America. Constructed around the classical epideictic mode, this eulogy, however, departed from the classical structure in the very many digressions (six to be exact) that assume such prominence and weight that we at times wonder, justly, whether the eulogy was merely a mask for a public appeal to redress the plight of black people in America. By beginning on a specific theme and then digressing to an individualistic and almost spontaneous tracing of an idea, the eulogy falls very much in the tradition of jazz where a melody is used as a springboard into digressive melodic explorations that are highly individualistic and spontaneous. This structural feature of digression was typical of the black eulogy of the nineteenth century, but Crummell's eulogy on Clarkson displayed this form par excellence.

Crummell's eulogy on Clarkson was not as philosophically reflective as his earlier eulogy on Sidney (1840), yet he did find the opportunity, while extolling Clarkson's political achievements, to refer to the ultimate goal of man. As he had done in his treatise on education, he bewailed "the brutality of animal passions" (202) and urged, instead, "noble aspirations after truth" (205). Underpinning his entire address was his appeal for a "spiritual purpose" (205) in all men's lives even as it was in Clarkson's life. Crummell held firm in his belief that "Everlasting Principles and Eternal Truth" (261) were truly present in an invisible world, and they guided men's actions. So real was this "Everlasting Truth" to Crummell that he experienced it like the physical laws of the universe: "TRUTH: an element more energetic than the elemental fires of earth; more potent than the gravitating force of the universe" (225). He exhorted his listeners to recognize that the greatness of Clarkson and all men of wisdom and goodwill stemmed from their fulfilling their human duty which was to pursue truth with unswerving zeal and to be guided by first principles. Crummell remained faithful to the ontological vision which he had developed in his Sidney eulogy as he indirectly appealed to his audience "to vindicate Truth; to uphold Principle; to walk steadfastly in the pathway of Duty" (228). It is noteworthy that, in eulogizing Clarkson whose greatest achievement was his role in the abolition of the slave trade, Crummell still did not veer into a strictly humanistic mold but kept his eyes fixed on the spiritual purpose behind this achievement. The essential thrust behind all blows against slavery was not the alleviating of human suffering but the glorification of God by doing what is right and true. Slavery obstructed the principle of unity, unity among mankind, and so to uphold this principle which was the duty of man to uphold, slavery must be struck down. Herein lay the grandeur of Thomas Clarkson. Impressed by "the hand of destiny, the finger of Providence" (212), he yielded to the "high guidance" (207). He allowed the intuitive truths to shine through, and though he was a brilliant scholar, he submitted to "the suggestions of the Divine Spirit" (220–221). This, indeed, was the essence of Crummell's concept of true wisdom; first, intense intellectual training and, then, a humble yielding to the intuitive truths which work on man. Thus, Crummell extolled Francis Bacon's wisdom as proceeding from a "human mind [which] in its excursions after Truth . . . [was given] the light of a single Principle" (259). So, too, Thomas Clarkson was described as a man who did exhaustive research on the subject of the slave trade, but, in the final analysis, his greatness issued from the fact that he "blind[ed] not the light vouchsafed him from on high" (207). There was almost the sound of wishful thinking as Crummell championed the truth of human brotherhood: "This is the age of BROTHERHOOD AND HUMANITY" (264). It is clear that the spiritual concerns of Crummell shone through, brightly and consistently, in his eulogy on Thomas Clarkson.

Right up to 1848, the year he left America for England, Crummell displayed a strong Pan–African identity. It was true that Crummell took a very strong anti–colonizationist stance in his 1847 treatise on education, and implicitly attacked the American Colonization Society in the Clarkson eulogy, yet, in this eulogy, he identified himself and all the black people in America as Africans. On more than one occasion in the eulogy, he spoke of "we, children of Africa in this land" (254, 260–261). Also, when he appealed for the "disenthralment of Africa," and the cause of the African race, various black nationalities did not define black people in Crummell's mind. When he considered the destined role of the black man in God's creation, Crummell spoke in terms of all black people, not just black Americans: "The Providences of God have placed the Negro race, before Europe and America, in the most commanding position"

(264). Whenever he mentioned the manifest destiny of black people, he always included all black people—those at home in Africa and those abroad in the New World. Toward the end of the Clarkson eulogy, he brought the whole Pan-African sweep of West Indian, American, and African blacks together as he saw the ultimate triumph of the black race "with the gifts of freedom vouchsafed us by the Almighty in this land, in part, and the West Indies . . . and the exceeding interest exhibited for Africa by her own children" (266).

The tensions set up, on the one hand, by Alexander Crummell's Pan-African concern and its contrary, a strong American nationalism, and, on the other hand, by his Christian idealism and its contrary, a steady eye on the pragmatic and practical concerns of the black man, generated the vitality and zealousness that defined his life. In his sermons, eulogies, and addresses, we see a Crummell deeply committed to the uplift of the black race, but he believed that westernized black missionaries and, more particularly, talented and educated black people had to bear the burden in elevating the race. At this point in his career, his Pan-African focus was on group solidarity among black Americans. Furthermore, this uplifting of black people must be founded on spiritual values, for superseding all else has to be the pursuit of Truth and the glorification of God.

2

Alexander Crummell in England

After his ordination by Bishop Lee in 1844, Crummell had difficult times. Times of "shades," he called them. For some time, he worked in an Episcopal parish in Providence, Rhode Island, but by 1845 he was rector of the Church of the Messiah in his native New York City. This church of the Messiah had had a checkered history. It was the outgrowth of the second Episcopal church in New York for black people, started by a black man, Mr. John Peterson, under the name of St. Matthew's Church. The Reverend Isaiah G. DeGrasse was its minister and later the Reverend Mr. Edward Jones; however, both men were so sorely discouraged by the almost impossible conditions from which to build a pastorate that they were forced to leave. There was no church building, and so church services had to be held in hired rooms; on several occasions, because of lack of funds to pay rent, services had to be suspended. When Crummell became minister, he was determined to build his own church, but his black parishioners were too poor and the white Episcopalians just did not care about their black brethren.[1] Actually, Crummell's aim to build a black church in New York was somewhat far-fetched, for he did not have enough parishioners to offer him a living. He, himself, testified that he almost died from starvation. It should be noted that the dry, bookish and intellectual quality of his sermons must have discouraged any swelling numbers at his diocese. Some of his sermons, like "Lecture on the Lord's Prayer," were dry exegeses on biblical texts, and even when he spoke of liberty, he spoke not of the oppressive conditions that were crushing his poor, black parishioners, but of "the Perfect Law of Liberty" as enunciated in the epistle of St. James.[2] His audiences must have shifted and turned uneasily in their seats and silently must have vowed to miss the next service. Thus, Crummell's parishioners were not only poor, but small in number. Mere physical survival was, indeed, a challenge for Crummell and his family.[3] Such was the state of affairs when Crummell set sail for England.

As early as July 15, 1845, there is evidence that Crummell was seeking to further his education at an English university, and two wealthy Englishwomen were willing to help defray the expenses for him and his wife.[4] It is not surprising, therefore, that in 1847, overwhelmed by the distresses and tribulations at the Church of the Messiah, he eagerly seized on the suggestion of some well-meaning white Episcopal clergymen[5] to go to England to raise funds to build a black church in New York. Even less surprising would be the detour he would take from his expressed fund-raising mission in order to attend Queen's College, Cambridge University. Crummell set sail for England at the beginning of 1848, and that same year a committee was formed "for the purpose of assisting the Reverend Alexander Crummell . . . to raise a sum of money for the purpose of building or purchasing a church in New York for the destitute Negro population of that city."[6] Included on the committee were the bishop of Bombay, the Right Reverend J. Harding and other prestigious ministers, and two accountants, R. B. Seeley, Esq., and John Labouchere, Esq.

Crummell's decision to seek support from Great

Britain was no unique undertaking.[7] Traditionally, Great Britain had many sympathetic friends to black Americans. As early as the eighteenth century, the child prodigy poet Phillis Wheatley was lionized in London.[8] In the early decades of the nineteenth century, Paul Cuffe visited England, and by the mid-nineteenth century, Frederick Douglass had to seek safety in England from "slave catchers" who were hot in pursuit of him after the publication of his famous autobiographical *Narrative of the Life of Frederick Douglass*. And it was to England that Douglass again fled when threatened with being arrested as an alleged accomplice to the courageous act of John Brown at Harper's Ferry. George Shepperson lists as visitors to Scotland on behalf of the antislavery cause over a dozen blacks, including Ira Aldridge, Samuel R. Ward, James McCune Smith, Douglass, Garnet, and Crummell.[9] As a matter of fact, in the 1840s and 1850s, many noted black Americans not only visited but resided in Great Britain for several months and even years. For example, Charles Lenox Remond in 1840 went as a delegate to the World's Anti-Slavery Convention in London but stayed on for two years. So, too, Frederick Douglass's 1845 visit to Great Britain lasted for nineteen months. William Wells Brown visited Paris in 1849 and actually spent five years and two months residing in various parts of Europe.[10] In 1855, Brown published *The American Fugitive in Europe* relating how well he was received in England: "In the British Museum and National Gallery . . . I had been treated as a man. The 'negro pew,' which I had seen in the churches of America, was not to be found in the churches of London. . . . [My daughters] had been received in the London schools upon terms of perfect equality."[11] Also, Samuel R. Ward noted in his *Autobiography* (1855) how generously the Scottish people responded to the antislavery cause. Thus, it became more and more common in the two decades preceding the Civil War for black leaders to seek escape from American racism and support for their abolitionist enterprises across the Atlantic Ocean. After the passage of the 1850 Fugitive Slave Act, the State Department had a busy time rejecting many applications by black leaders for passports to England.[12] Frederick Douglass best summed up the mood of exile and migration in the 1850s: "The night is a dark and stormy one. We have lost some of our strong men."[13] Douglass went on to list Ward, Brown, Longuen, Garnet, and Crummell as some of the strong black men who might never return to America. Douglass's fear was misplaced, for they all finally returned, though Crummell after an absence of nearly thirty years. Thus, when Crummell arrived in England on January 26, 1848, he had become part of the procession of those black "ministers without portfolio" to the British Isles.

In England, Crummell pursued his fund-raising mission with his usual diligence. Douglass's *North Star* reported Crummell's preaching two sermons on one Sunday (in the morning at St. Silas's Church and in the evening at St. Luke's) both with the approval of the Lord Bishop of Chester. On another Sunday, in the morning he read prayers at St. Silas's Church, in the afternoon he preached at Waliasey Church (£11 10s were collected), and in the evening he preached at Christ Church. Douglass noted the "talent, unobtrusive work and piety" of the Reverend Mr. Crummell and applauded his efforts to heal his twenty thousand brethren in New York.[14] Crummell's mission was endorsed by the highest echelons in the Anglican church in England, and several English newspapers carried accounts of his addresses and appeals for funds.

From the spring of 1848 to the fall of 1851, he assiduously employed himself in raising funds. He preached in London, Liverpool, Birmingham, Manchester, Bath, and Gloucester and succeeded in raising £1,934 6s 3d. From this grand total, £358 10s 4d were given to him for personal expenses which included day–to–day living expenses, travel, printing of material, and so forth; £1,400 were duly deposited in a bank until land on which to build a church could be purchased, and the rest of the money was given to him to help further his education.[15] More than forty years later in his Jubilate address, Crummell proudly noted that the money he had collected in England, though it never built the church for which it was earmarked, became "a part of the ENDOWMENT of St. Phillip's [Colored] Church, in [New York], yielding annually the sum of $373.50."[16]

Furthering his education was always part of the purpose of Crummell's going to England. The bishops of London, Oxford, and Norwich had all supported the idea of an English university education for Crummell, and the Reverend Henry Caswell, an Englishman, had expressed a willingness to raise funds to help Crummell pursue a university education.[17] Crummell felt particularly pleased to get the opportunity to study at Cambridge University. Some years earlier (1846), in his eulogium on Thomas Clarkson, the young orator had spoken in glowing terms about Cambridge University's contribution "to the cause of piety, religious reformation, philanthropy and freedom."[18] He had marveled at the long list of distinguished men including Bacon, Milton, Newton, Latimer, Cranmer, George Herbert, Wilberforce, and Clarkson who had been educated at Cambridge University, and now he was being given the opportunity to walk the same hallowed halls as these celebrated scholars. Crummell had to be particularly pleased to study at Cambridge University which had a reputation for promoting and defending freedom for all human beings. He himself had once declared, "No seat of learning in the world has done more, for human liberty and human well–being, than this institution [Cambridge University]."[19]

He became a resident of Queen's College probably in 1850 while he was still raising funds to build a church in New York. He took his Previous (Preliminary) Examination in the Lent term, 1851, and passed in the second class which granted him a certificate of approval to pursue studies for the ordinary degree. To pass his Previous, Crummell had to study one of the four Gospels in the original Greek, master Old Testament history and Paley's *Evidences of Christianity,* read closely in the original one Greek and one Latin classic, and have a good working knowledge of elementary geometry and arithmetic.[20] For his B.A. degree, Crummell studied mathematics, classics, and divinity. He took his finals in January 1853 but had to take them again the following month before he was finally granted the B.A.[21] This rigorous training prepared Crummell to become a college professor at Liberia College; moreover, so respected was his learning in theology that he was advising on the matter of transubstantiation and Holy Communion during the final weeks of his life.[22] His mastery of Greek and Latin enabled Crummell, many years later, to ridicule Senator Calhoun, who said a black man would never be able to conjugate a Latin verb or decline a Greek noun.[23]

Underlying most of Crummell's speeches in England were his beliefs in the fundamental principle of unity, which he had articulated in his Sidney eulogy, and the spiritual end of man, which was central to all his ideas on any subject. For example, to persuade his English audiences of the urgent need for black churches in America, Crummell pointed out that the American republic lacked the spirit of brotherhood (principle of unity), and he insisted that, "Until the Negro race were raised up and received as brethren, both [black and white Americans] would remain unhealthy and incomplete."[24] The spiritual health of America (the spiritual end of man) also had to be measured by the condition of the black man: "[Black Americans] would ever be the criterion of the American religion."[25] The Jim Crow attitudes in American churches and the shutting of many seminaries to aspiring black ministers exhibited the spiritual sickness of America. In this way, by appealing to the principle of unity and the spiritual end of man, Crummell urged his English listeners to contribute to the building of a black church in New York.

More pertinent to us than Crummell's fundraising efforts and university education was the affirmation of his Pan-African vision as formulated in several of his speeches. Again, the principle of unity and the spiritual end of man shaped his vision. Crummell's Pan-African position rested on three premises: first and foremost, the idea of racial solidarity among black people wherever they may be (the principle of unity); second, his belief that each race had characteristics peculiarly suited to itself; and third, the rightness of Christian civilization (the spiritual end of man) to guide the race to a glorious future.

Crummell accepted an invitation to address "The Ladies' Negro Educational Society," an organization established in England for the education of black people in the British West Indies. He demonstrated his solidarity with black people, whether West Indian, American, or whatever nationality, by identifying completely with this West Indian organization: "I feel [that to advocate the claims of the Society] . . . is . . . to plead for my own life and blood, and to vindicate my own personal interests and advantages."[26] In England, Crummell was becoming a greater advocate for black international unity than he had been in America. He seized the opportunity to recognize publicly before a group of black people from the West Indies that black people in America and in the West Indies shared common interests. His commitment to Pan-African solidarity did not allow

him to accept any black organization that did not
have as its goal, "to raise up the great African
family, in its several sections, to civilization and
enlightenment."[27] When he spoke, he addressed not
West Indian black people but "the Negro race, . . .
scattered abroad through the world, as well as
dwelling in their homes in Africa."[28] It is interesting to note that in the year of his arrival in England (1848), Crummell was still narrowly Afro-
American in his outlook: "I am identified with my
race in America in all their trials, sufferings, struggles, hopes, aspirations, and endeavors."[29] Nothing is
really wrong with this sentiment except that
Crummell seemed to reserve his compassion for only
black Americans. Three years later, Crummell had
become more conscious of Africa as his field of work:
"There is no spot, of all this wide world, to which my
heart travels with more ardent affection than Africa
. . . although born in the United States, . . . I should
think myself privileged . . . [to spend] the small
measure of [my] ability . . . in efforts for the salvation of those to whom I am connected by descent in
that benighted land."[30] Crummell was now an
internationlist in his Pan–African concerns. Away
from the particular problems of Afro–Americans,
Crummell became more convinced that Africans in
Africa and abroad were one people with one destiny.
"One Aim! One Goal! One Destiny!"

This spirited appeal for international Pan–African
unity was really a plea for black people to close ranks
against scurrilous attacks on the African race. In
England, Crummell had found attacks, similar to
those he had known in America, directed against the
integrity of the black man. Ironically, the most
notorious attack came from the pen of Thomas
Carlyle whose philosophy of life Crummell shared.
Carlyle had condemned the materialistic beliefs of
the nineteenth century in his work *Signs of the Times,*
and he had preached that the ultimate course

of the universe was spiritual. Crummell clearly
shared this belief in the supremacy of the spiritual
world; moreover, as expressed in *Sartor Resartus,*
Carlyle's belief that all mankind was divine echoed
Crummell's belief in the divine principle working
through all men. Yet, in his infamous essay on "The
Nigger Question," (1849) Carlyle denied the black
man's having any intellectual worth, and he argued
that the emancipation of black people from slavery
would lead to general depravity.[31] Crummell realized
that when Carlyle had written about "the
God–created Form" which lay in the poor laborer
toiling unnoticed, he was not including the black
laborer who toiled on the slave plantations. William
Wells Brown, who was also in England at the time of
Carlyle's "Nigger Question," published an opinion on
Carlyle which he could have first discussed with
Crummell when he had visited him at Cambridge
University: "His [Carlyle's] recent attack upon the
emancipated people of the West Indies, and his
laborious article in favor of the reestablishment of
the lash and slavery, had created in my mind a dislike
for the man."[32] Brown went on to admit that in some
things Carlyle was right "but in many he is entirely
wrong." Though Carlyle did not necessarily represent
the pervading attitude in England at the time towards
blacks, the fact is that the former enthusiasm of
Clarkson and Wilberforce for the interests of black
people was on the wane. Thus, when a letter appeared
in the London *Christian Observer* in 1850 suggesting
that God had created the black man to be forever a
slave, Crummell took time off from his fund–raising
lectures to deliver an address, "The Negro Race Not
Under a Curse."[33]

Defense of the African race was certainly a phase
in the early Pan–African movement. The prevailing
argument during the mid–nineteenth century was that
God had put a curse on black people, condemning
them throughout the ages to be "hewers of wood and

drawers of water." Nineteenth–century black intellectuals never had accepted these allegations which
were posited as explanations for the enslavement and
oppression of black people. These intellectuals tended
to recognize two pasts for Africa—the immediate
past which was cruel, repulsive, and bloody with
slavery, and a remote past which was glorious and
filled with grandeur and wisdom. The puzzling question was—what happened? How and when did the
grandeur that was Africa's pass away? Unable to
account for this dramatic change, these black
intellectuals devoted much time and energy exposing
the fallacies and inconsistencies in the various theo-
ries about the black race. Crummell set out in his
1850 lecture to expose the errors in the biblical argument which presented the black race as a cursed
race. He accepted the myth of a divine curse, but he
simply shifted the burden onto another race. He
never doubted that the native African needed to be
enlightened, for, not having the benefit of
twentieth–century sociological and anthropological
insights, Crummell failed to recognize the com-
plexity and sophistication of African societies. He
uncritically believed that Christian values superseded
all other values and condemned polygamy and African
religious practices as barbaric.

To offset what he saw as "the backward state" of
native Africans, Crummell encouraged Pan–African
solidarity by tracing the relatively recent achievements of black people like Anthony Amo* and
Toussaint L'Ouverture, and he proudly pointed to the
developing nation–states of Sierra Leone and Liberia.
Yet the question remained: if not a curse, why the
enslaved condition of black people? Guided by his

---

*An African from Guinea who had earned a Ph.D.
from the University of Wittenberg in the eighteenth
century.

belief in divine determinism, Crummell could not even think along the lines of economic exploitation. To accept that God decreed black labor for capitalistic development was to agree with the hewers-of-wood theory. He rationalized the enslavement of black people by resorting to the general principle that only through suffering could greatness be achieved. Moreover, the enlightenment of the descendants of slaves equipped them to return to their motherland and help in the regeneration of Africa. Crummell never addressed the question of the fall of ancient Africa from her pinnacle of glory. Yet, he never doubted that Africa once enjoyed a golden age of wisdom, and he urged Pan-African unity as a means to help "Ethiopia" once again stretch forth her hands in glory.

This appeal for an international racial solidarity was part of Crummell's Pan-African ideology before he left America. In England, however, his international Pan-African dream began to take definite shape. He proposed the theory that each race had its own peculiar genius, and quite naturally expected the Pan-African movement to be grounded on the peculiar genius of the African race. He never argued that the peculiar characteristics of a race were biologically or genetically inherited; in fact, he never suggested that they were characteristics that only one race had. Rather, all races shared common characteristics, but a particular race, for whatever reasons, might show a greater tendency than other races to a particular set of characteristics. Within Crummell's ontology, these peculiar abilities were divinely predetermined for the betterment of all mankind. In the case of the African race, Crummell identified the spiritual tendency as its peculiar genius. As he put it: "Religious susceptibility and moral dispositions are the more marked characteristics of the Negro family, and the main point wherein they differ from other races."[34] Crummell was obviously using his personal tendencies and experiences as the measuring rod for the entire race. Since he was an Episcopal minister, he could best pursue his Pan-African quest along religious paths. He translated his personal bias into innate racial tendencies. Besides, this "religious susceptibility" conveniently fitted the oppressed condition of the black man, for, religion, in Crummell's view, pointed the way toward "inward, spiritual rest."[35] Not even good works were as meaningful as this inborn tendency toward the spiritual end of man: "Good works may serve as evidence of our faith but never as instruments for our salvation."[36] Clearly, Crummell was moving toward the position that the black race by virtue of its God-given "susceptibility" was a chosen race. He elaborated upon the African's unique genius by proclaiming that the native African was always yearning for a "higher religion."[37]

For Crummell, this "higher religion" meant Christianity. Of crucial importance in understanding Crummell's thinking is his meaning of the word "higher." He did not deny that native Africans had their own religious practices, for he had argued that the African race was marked by "religious susceptibility." However, Crummell had been imbued with and had accepted the values of *Christian* western civilization. These western values he proposed as the goal to be achieved by Africans. He unquestioningly believed in western classical wisdom and Christianity as developed in the western world. Consequently, without ever having been to Africa, he felt that whatever religious customs the African was practicing were "backward," and, in order that their innate spiritual tendencies be most effectively developed, they needed Christian enlightenment. He saw Pan-African progress in the many Christian ministers and teachers in the West Indies and along the coast and in the interior of Africa. However, the core of Pan-African unity was the native African, so

Crummell, while in England, encouraged the training of native priests and teachers. African kings, princes, and chiefs wanted their children and subjects instructed in Christianity, and Crummell predicted that soon "the days of Cyprian and Augustine shall again return to Africa."[38] For Crummell, aristocracy determined worth, and kings, princes, and chiefs defined what was best for a people. The best unity was vertical—from the top down. Spiritualization meant the Christian faith. Thus, Crummell, steeped in western classical learning and trained as a Christian minister, went to Africa as a missionary, as someone who considered himself to be on a superior level reaching down to help his benighted brothers. The Pan–African brotherhood he sought to develop was deeply grounded in the Christian faith as the external manifestation of the African's "religious susceptibility."

England had opened Crummell's eyes to the world at large. While in England, he visited some of the noblest families and most famous personages of Great Britain. He met and became a close friend of the widow of the great abolitionist Thomas Clarkson whom he had eulogized as a young man in his twenties. He also became a close friend of the former mayor of Bath, Mr. William T. Blair, who actually handled Crummell's financial affairs in England when he went to Liberia to live. So well–liked and respected was Crummell that a Bishop Hinds licensed him to a curacy at Ipswich for six months. Crummell was overwhelmed by the distinguished families who entertained him in their homes. He recalled listening, at the home of one of these families, "to that brilliant avalanche of history and biography, of poetry and criticism which rushed from the brain and lips of Thomas Babington Macaulay."[39]

Many black Americans, dating back to Phillis Wheatley in the eighteenth century, reveled in the fact that, whereas in America they could not ride a streetcar without being disgraced, in England they were lionized and entertained at the tables of some of the most famous Englishmen. William Wells Brown wrote proudly that "I had eaten at the same table with Sir Edward Bulwer Lytton, Charles Dickens, Eliza Cook, Alfred Tennyson, and the son–in–law of Sir Walter Scott."[40] In fact, Brown had felt comfortable and secure enough to express dislike at having to ride on the same omnibus as Thomas Carlyle![41] Undoubtedly recalling his treatment at the hands of Bishop Onderdonk and the racist American prelates and clergymen, Crummell happily reported the public support he received from, among others, the dean of St. Paul's, Dr. Thirwell, the bishop of London, Dr. Blomfield, and the lord of Norwich, Dr. Stanley. He also proudly recalled dining with noted English families like the Froudes, the Thackerays, and the Patmores. Throughout his life he treasured as dear friends the Reverend Henry Venn, the Reverend Henry Caswell, and other English clergymen.

Crummell's high praise for English liberalism displayed a rather naïve perception of the true state of affairs on the matter of race among the English elite. Carlyle was not an errant intellectual with a blind spot for racism; rather, he was the culmination of a mid–nineteenth century trend in England against the liberation of black people.[42] Thomas Babington Macaulay, the distinguished historian with whom Crummell proudly reported he had dined, only three years before Crummell's arrival in England had openly and unambiguously supported slavery.[43] James Anthony Froude, another brilliant Englishman of letters whose acquaintance Crummell treasured throughout his life, became a notorious defender of slavery.[44] At the time of his Jubilate address when Crummell was recounting with fond memories his meeting with Froude, the Regius Professor of Modern History at Oxford University had already published his racist tract, *The English in the West Indies,* and, more importantly, J. J. Thomas, a West Indian of pure African descent had answered Froude's follies and fallacies in a remarkable work entitled *Froudacity*. [45] According to the historian Eric Williams, Coleridge, Wordsworth, Wilberforce, and even Clarkson were tarnished by inconsistent stands on the matter of slavery. [46]

Either Crummell was ignorant of the short-comings of the English liberals, or he chose to close his eyes to English racism in order to court friendship across the Atlantic in battling American racism. In any case, his Talented Tenth mentality fit in well with the elitist values that permeated English society, and Crummell carried with him till his death a deep respect and reverence for almost anything English. Nearly thirty years later, when he sought a model for a church he was building, he went to England. He kept up a steady correspondence with his English friends who supported him during difficult times in Liberia. He even tended to favor some English-trained black West Indians above black Americans, and, during the last years of his life, one of his black West Indian connections was England-based Sylvester Williams[47] who, no doubt prompted by Crummell and his American Negro Academy, called the first formal Pan-African Conference in 1900.

All in all, Crummell's time in England was a period of intellectual growth and exposure to some of the best minds and most influential men of the mid-nineteenth century. Crummell summed it up best: "My five years' residence in England was, save the interruptions of sickness, a period of grand opportunities, of the richest privileges, of cherished remembrances and golden light."[48]

Sickness was the one glum note that sounded during Crummell's stay in England. Actually, sickness was a grim companion of Crummell's throughout his life. It was sickness, in part, that motivated his traveling to England. While in England, he was under the care of one of England's most famous physicians at the time, Sir Benjamin Brodie. Sir Benjamin urged Crummell to seek a warmer climate, in Africa, but Liberia, with its then notorious malaria fever, was a curious choice for health reasons.

Yet Sir Benjamin might have been thinking of Crummell's psychological health. In 1847 Liberia had become an independent nation, and, though America did not formally acknowledge this independence until 1862, in the early 1850s Liberia's future seemed bright. Within the context of an independent black nation, Crummell, with an academic and religious training that placed him head and shoulders above most black men of the age let alone the Liberian settlers, could become a dominating force in shaping the redemption of Africa. It was being rumored that, once in Liberia, he would become the first black Episcopalian bishop,[49] and, who knows, as William Wells Brown speculated, "We should not be surprised if he became president of Liberia."[50]

To quiet all speculations about any political ambitions, Crummell declared that he would keep himself "entirely abstinent of politics," and offered to go to Liberia as an unsalaried missionary, "to set up a school."[51] The Foreign Mission*, however, offered Crummell a salaried appointment as a missionary in Liberia, and he eagerly accepted the job with one regret, "I have not my full physical powers to give to the cause."[52] "The cause," as Crummell termed it, was the building of a great nation in Africa comprised of a Pan–African cross section of black people from Africa, America, and the West Indies. The

---

*The Foreign Mission, also described as the African Mission, referred to the foreign arm of the Domestic and Foreign Missionary Society in America. The committee which supervised the Foreign Mission was called the Foreign Committee.

architects and chief builders of this new Pan–African nation would be the educated middle class who, with their western learning and Christian ideals, would lift up the masses of native Africans from their benighted condition. At least, so thought the still somewhat immature Crummell.

3

Alexander Crummell: Missionary in Liberia

Crummell, along with his wife and five children, set sail from Plymouth, England, on June 24, 1853, and arrived at Monrovia, Liberia, on August 8, 1853.[1] Three days after his arrival, his "governmental indifference vanished," and he applied for citizenship papers.[2] This did not mean that he had surrendered his role as missionary, but it did show that he intended to become part of the the destiny of Liberia. He was no foreign missionary who had come only to save the natives' souls; he was putting down his roots in African soil. Crummell was staking out his future in Liberia.

He earnestly believed that the redemption of Africa was at hand, and with the establishment of the black, independent Liberian nation, he saw the beginning of the restoration of black people to their former place of eminence among the other peoples on earth. "On the continent of Africa," he preached, "a civilization, of a new type, and more noble and more glorious, in some of its features, than as ever before existed, is on the eve of starting into life."[3] Confident in his belief that a new day was at hand for black people and that Ethiopia was about to stretch forth her hand once more, his first impressions of Africa were seen through romantic glasses. Sierra Leone became in his optimistic eyes a veritable Eden with majestic forests, multitudinous and varied animals and "most interesting" people. The Timmanees, his father's tribe, displayed "nobility of character [and an] indomitable spirit and unconquerable [mind]." He marveled at the physical beauty of the African and the "mental and real genius" of the Mandingoes.[4] Liberia, in particular, showed much promise, and he praised the thrift, the energy, and the spirit of national life that pervaded this young nation.[5] He saw Liberia as more than a place of refuge for black people from oppression and slavery. This young black nation had set new and higher standards for the world: "The world *needs* a higher type of true nationality than it now has: why should not we [Liberians] furnish it? . . . Why not make ourselves a precedent?"[6]

By "a higher type of true nationality," this young optimistic clergyman had in mind a nation that reflected the ways and workings of the Absolute: "The workings of our political institutions . . . and the movements of society . . . must be as exact and as beautiful as the ways of nature, if we retain hearts and wills in unison with that ONE great heart and will which equally guides a planet and starts the pulsations of our veins."[7] The practical affairs of state must fall in line with the will that guided the affairs of the universe. Crummell saw no dichotomy between the practical and the ideal, the pragmatic and the mystical. The practical world of materialism should be nothing more than a manifestation of the spiritual world of idealism. He saw no inconsistency nor conflict in mystical meditation and practical affairs of the world. Indeed, the one was contingent on the other. Since all nature was an external manifestation of the mystical ways of God, Crummell did not dismiss this third-dimensional world as a falsity, a mere imitation of reality. This tangible, physical world was, for him, an externalization, almost an extension of the ideal world, and as such it was not counterfeit but real. Reality had two facets to it: one was a reality made up of phenomena, the other was a reality of noumena. When man, therefore, constructed his world of phenomena—political institutions, commercial enterprises, agricultural industries, and so forth—he should seek to imitate the world of natural phenomena—the movement of the planets, the pulsations of the blood. His nation was conceived as a nation of God. In forthright language he urged, "Let God be our Governor,"[8] and he warned that "the powers that be are ordained of God."[9]

Though Crummell saw that the true possibility of mankind lay more in the mystical world of Christian principles than in the busy world of industry and commerce, it was the busy world of practical affairs that dominated most of his life in Liberia. For example, in his very first letter soon after his arrival in Liberia, he expressed concern that a church needed to be built "at once" in Monrovia.[10] Though he had come to Liberia as a missionary on a spiritual mission, one of his first efforts was directed to the practical matter of erecting a church.

The establishment of a church became central to the Christian Pan-African concept. The permanent concrete structure of a church took on almost symbolic proportions in Crummell's life. In America, he had seen the need for black people to own their own church in which they could congregate and worship. He knew that traditionally the church had provided the meeting place for black unity. Accordingly, to implement his Pan-African dream, he became obsessed with the idea of building a church in Monrovia. In his early letters, he repeated *ad nauseam* his request for the erection of a church building: "I cannot tell you how important it is that a church—not a school room or a lecture room—but a *church* should be erected in this town [Monrovia] at the earliest possible period."[11] Should he not survive the acclimatizing phase in Liberia, he begged but one favor: "I beg to call your attention to the absolute need of a good church edifice in this town [Monrovia]."[12] So single–minded was he in his determination to have a church built in Monrovia that by November 11, 1854, he could happily report, "The church edifice's foundation . . . [is] . . . almost all laid down."[13] However, two weeks later he was complaining that work on the church "will regretfully have to stop" because of too great expenses! Obviously, this sudden turn around in two weeks reflects poor budget planning on the young missionary's part. This inability to oversee financial matters effectively both in his private and public life was one of the major flaws in Crummell's character.

The project for erecting a church building led to his resignation from the Foreign Mission. Crummell raised funds among his English friends, but the expenses continued to grow and the overrun was upward of $10,000.[14] His old friend and advisor, Dr. Tyng of Washington, D.C., made a generous donation to the building of the church, and a committee was appointed with Crummell as secretary and architect to oversee the day–by–day construction. The handling of the funds was taken out of his control, and the home office wrote Crummell inquiring about records concerning the church expenses which they had never received. When he submitted his records, it was found that he had overdrawn his account. Crummell may have felt that his honesty was being questioned, especially when his bishop in Liberia directed him to send extracts of his diary. Moreover, the bishop decided to cut Crummell's salary by $100. That was the final straw. On October 8, 1856, Crummell wrote to Secretary Irving at the home office of the Foreign Mission: "I cannot commence a new year, in charge of the station at Monrovia, at the salary of $850 a year." He also wrote to the bishop of this same concern, adding, "I would have to resort to some secular pursuit." However, when the officers of the Foreign

Mission Committee met in early 1857 to consider Crummell's case, after reviewing his overdrawn accounts and his apparent lack of effectiveness against Eli Stokes, a black minister who was winning widespread support in his campaign for an independent black church, they turned down his request for a salary increase. Crummell had no choice but to resign. In March 1857, he wrote the home office, "With regret and painful disappointment ... I close my correspondence with your office with my best wishes for the success and progress of the church's work on this coast." The church building project had proved to be his undoing, and even though he did rejoin the Foreign Mission, no mention was made in any of his correspondence about the completion and final opening of Trinity Church in Monrovia.

The Reverend Dr. Caswell, English secretary for the West Indian Mission on the River Pangas in Sierra Leone, did not allow Crummell's resignation to go unnoticed. Caswell wrote to the American Foreign Mission indicating his willingness to have the American Episcopal priest join the West Indian Mission. However, Caswell pointed out that an American missionary would be more effective in Liberia, and if money was the problem the English would be willing to pay the difference in Crummell's salary to have him maintained in Liberia. Caswell went so far as to suggest that the Liberian Mission could be transferred to the West Indian Mission if the problem was with the bishop in Liberia. The English missionary further pointed out that Stokes' popularity was due to his African nationalism, while Crummell loyally preferred to maintain American links. In any case, the English were determined to keep Crummell in West Africa, either in Liberia or with the West Indian Mission in Sierra Leone.[15] The board of the Foreign Mission took the letter under advisement. A tidy solution was found to keep Crummell in Liberia. Since a college was soon to be established in Liberia, he could have a position there. The Foreign Committee could maintain him as a missionary and allow him to be an instructor at the new college.[16] There is evidence that by July 1858 Crummell was back with the Foreign Mission though he was now stationed at Mount Vaughan.[17] In the interim, between his resignation and his reappointment with the Foreign Mission, it seems that Crummell was a missionary at St. John's Church, in the Maryland Colony which had been annexed to Liberia in 1857.

At Mount Vaughan, Crummell seemed more settled. He was in charge of a boys' high school, and his correspondence took the form of requests for books and school supplies and scholarships for promising students. He also established several stations toward the interior, and his missionary work was centered among the native Africans. This closer association with native Africans proved, later on, to be very significant in modifying Crummell's concept of the role of the masses in the Pan-African movement. In 1858, he planned an expedition up the St. Paul's River with the intention of getting an accurate description of the valley of that river complete with a correct map and a recording of views of interesting objects.[18] The year before there had been something of a famine in Liberia,[19] and he might have been addressing this practical problem when he planned this expeditionary trip. The missionary must not only pray, he must also direct his attention toward practical affairs. It was this missionary activity in the secular affairs of the state that no doubt prompted William Nesbit, a black American who visited Liberia in 1855, to claim: "[The missionaries] have really done nothing in the way of civilizing and christianizing Africa."[20] But Mr. Nesbit was merely overstating his prejudices; Mr. Samuel Williams, a fellow black American who made the trip to Liberia on the same ship as Nesbit, offered a more balanced viewpoint when he stated that the missionaries in Liberia were "as upright as anywhere in the world,"[21] but Williams conceded that "they (the missionaries) have a tough fight against superstitions."[22] In fact, Crummell was establishing himself more as an educator and missionary than as an entrepreneur. Harriet G. Brittan, an Englishwoman who did missionary work for a year in Liberia in 1860, recalled in her diary having met the Reverend and Mrs. Crummell, and in addition to praising their refinement and good manners, she noted, "Poor Mr. Thompson! He is so anxious to enter the ministry, and he was studying so hard with Mr. Crummell."[23] This was the true Mr. Crummell—a devoted minister who exacted discipline and hard work from any young Liberian aspiring for the priesthood. But he did not restrict his activities to explorations and teaching. His bad experience with the church building in Monrovia had not killed his enthusiasm for establishing a concrete structure, for, with the aid of the same reliable Dr. Tyng who had helped out with the Monrovia building, he built a church and school at Caldwell in which young men were trained for the priesthood.[24] It was probably here that Crummell trained his own son to be a minister.

Crummell's resignation from the Foreign Mission had gone contrary to his Pan–African plans. He had come to Liberia eager to offer, in the ecclesiastical sphere, the black leadership that the nation enjoyed in the political arena. He had understood that there could be no effective Christian Pan–African movement unless black people assumed the highest leadership roles in the state and the church. But the loyal Episcopal clergyman was not prepared to go all the way and establish an independent black church in Liberia. In America, he had never joined the independent black church which the Reverend Richard Allen had founded, but had chosen to remain within the structure of the Episcopal church. His goal was only a black congregation, in its own church building, governed by black people, but still under the umbrella of the Episcopal hierarchy, even as the Episcopal church enjoyed autonomy while still under the aegis of the Anglican church. In matters of doctrinal substance, he accepted Episcopal authority, but in the matter of local governance, he sought black control. Actually, it would have been inconsistent with Crummell's "principle of oneness" for him to have chosen to separate from the traditional hierarchical structure of the Episcopal/Anglican church. More consistent with his philosophy of unity would be ecumenical union rather than separation into a new Christian denomination. Thus, in Liberia he sought black control of the Episcopal church as opposed to establishing a separate black church. When, therefore, another black minister, Eli Stokes, backed by the bishop of Glasgow and other Scottish ecclesiastics, sought to bring together various black ministers from various Christian denominations and establish an independent black church in Liberia, Crummell stubbornly resisted his effort. The Liberian population, flush with its newly won national independence, was amenable to the idea of a religious independence commensurate with its political status, and, in large numbers, they rallied around Stokes. Crummell either misread Stokes's popularity, mistaking the Methodist minister's aggressive African nationalistic approach as mere mischief-making by a "pest,"[25] or he allowed himself to be blinded by his personal dislike of Stokes whom he described as "the most painstaking deceiver and liar that I ever met with."[26] In either case, Crummell, without offering a serious challenge, allowed Stokes to win over a greater proportion of the Liberian population. Had Crummell pursued a more independent nationalistic approach, his Pan-African movement might have been better served. But his conservative approach sought a limited measure of black autonomy within the existing Episcopal church organization.

A recent graduate of Cambridge University and a loyal Episcopal clergyman, Crummell had come to Africa with the expectation that he would become bishop of the Episcopal church in Liberia and so provide the Christian moral leadership for the Pan-African movement. Though no firm commitment had been made, an influential clergyman in New York had suggested the possibility of his becoming bishop.[27] But Crummell met a formidable obstruction in his pathway to the bishopric—Bishop John Payne.

The Reverend John Payne, a white missionary in Liberia, was appointed bishop of this newly independent black nation two years before Crummell's arrival in Africa. It was natural to expect that the Liberians, in the wake of the political privileges that national independence brought to them, would want corresponding ecclesiastical rights. Whether or not Bishop Payne heard rumors that a young, black Cambridge University graduate was being sent to take over the Episcopal bishopric in Liberia,[28] the bishop make a bold move to stop that possibility. In 1853, but before Crummell's arrival, the bishop urged the black clergy to establish a separate church organization in Liberia. However, he proposed forty years of foreign control of the church. To a man, the Liberian clergy rejected this idea of "gradual independence."[29] The Liberian citizens were obviously determined to secure their independence on all fronts, free of any paternalistic tarnish. It is against this background that Crummell's struggle with Bishop Payne over control of the Liberian Episcopal church must be examined.

Though personal ambition might have motivated Crummell's battles with Bishop Payne, his overriding concern was to ensure black leadership for black people. Even before he had left England, the black missionary began what was to become a litany of complaints against Bishop Payne. "I have nothing from Bishop Payne," he wrote to the American headquarters after he had sent his letter of appointment to the African Mission at Cape Palmas to Bishop Payne. Then, in his first letter from Africa, he repeated the fact that he had never received a reply from the bishop and in an impatient tone reported that since his arrival he had been instructed to "remain here [Monrovia] until the Bishop makes his visitation in September or October."[30] In this same letter, Crummell, after apologizing for giving his opinion before he had spoken with Bishop Payne, went on to offer "privately" his observations about the state of affairs in Monrovia. His private opinion implied that Bishop Payne was woefully neglecting his duties in Monrovia. Crummell wrote about his aiding two young men with their theological studies, then slyly added: "I hope the aid I am giving them will not be displeasing to the Bishop." He went on to report that several persons, even Methodists, wanted to be converted, but the lay reader had to wait for the bishop. In October, he was still complaining that Bishop Payne did visit the capital city but had ordered him to stay in Monrovia. The climate in Monrovia was more conducive to the dreaded malaria fever than the climate in Cape Palmas, and Crummell may have felt the bishop was deliberately exposing him and his family to the worst climate in order to discourage his staying in Liberia.

On March 28, 1854, responding to a request from the American headquarters for a statement concerning a prospective minister whom Bishop Payne did not want sent to the African Mission, Crummell recounted how Bishop Payne had flatly condemned the man, but that he himself could offer no opinion on the young man. Then, as if in a polite afterthought, he went on to wish the young minister well and to observe that every minister was needed in Africa.[31] Crummell might have vowed to keep clear of secular politics, but he was certainly involved in church politics and was not without ambitions to become bishop in Liberia.

Bishop Payne was determined to drive Crummell from Liberia; Crummell was determined to stay. In the midst of personal hardship, Crummell kept up his struggle with the bishop. From the earliest days, the dreaded malaria fever was ravishing Crummell's family. Within four months of his arrival at Monrovia, his youngest daughter, yet an infant, died of the fever, and on several occasions throughout his first year in Liberia, he expressed doubts about his wife's surviving the fever. Her health kept deteriorating for the first eight months of the acclimatizing phase, and Crummell felt that she might have to go to a temperate climate in the United States or England to save her life. But the determined clergyman was unyielding in his struggle with the bishop, "If she must go, I must stay."[32] The only concession he made to his wife's poor health was to spend two months in Cape Palmas where the weather was discernibly healthier.[33] His wife's health never seemed to improve, and three years later he was writing, "Again, and again and again, during the last two years, she has been seemingly at the point of death."[34] While his family around him struggled to survive the ravages of the fever, Crummell seemed to thrive on his battle with the bishop. Hardly a year beyond his arrival in Liberia he could write, "I think I shall have better health here than I have had in all my previous life."[35] When his father wrote expressing a desire to return to his African homeland, Crummell felt that "in his extreme old age . . . he could not stand the acclimation."[36] This sentiment might be quite true, yet the almost stoical indifference that he displayed in his letters concerning his wife's health, and the fact that in 1867 he did have his American–born mother, "going on ninety," living with him in Liberia, lead one to suspect that the struggle for the bishopric took precedence over his father's desire.

In addition to problems of family health, on January 11, 1855, fire destroyed Crummell's residence and left him and his family destitute. He had to move to a settlement further up the St. Paul's River, but he made regular visitations to his Monrovia parish. To alleviate the stress of too much traveling and to cut down on expenses, he took up a home in Monrovia at $175 a year. Bishop Payne saw his opportunity to separate Crummell from his thriving Trinity parish in Monrovia and from the erection of the church building which was in full gear, and he objected to Crummell's new Monrovian residence. In a letter to Secretary Irving of the Foreign Mission, Crummell pointed out the hardships of traveling along the St. Paul's during the rainy season, and he argued that to keep up services in Monrovia only on weekends would incur expenses in excess of $175 per annum. He was determined not to surrender his Trinity parish in Monrovia, certainly not before his church was built. Meanwhile, the church building expenses were growing, and Bishop Payne succeeded in creating apprehension among the authorities at the American home office. This initial clash with the bishop culminated in Crummell's resignation and subsequent reappointment to a teaching post at Mount Vaughan, Cape Palmas. Bishop Payne had clearly won the first battle, but Crummell held firm in his conviction to remain in Liberia and fight the white bishop.

Eli Stokes's success among the Liberians had made a marked impression on the home office of the Foreign Mission. In accepting Crummell's resignation, the directors at the home office had compared their Episcopal missionary unfavorably with Stokes who had support from Scottish churchmen. Yet, as Dr. Caswell had pointed out, Stokes's popularity rested largely on his nationalistic appeal for an independent Liberian church. Instead of being supported by his American superiors for his loyalty to the American

Episcopal church, Crummell was being put down. There was a lesson in this experience for the young black clergyman: An alliance with the working masses, as Stokes had sought, had more substance and worth than any cooperative venture with the ruling class, especially if the masses were black and the rulers, white. Stung by the ingratitude of the executive officers of the Foreign Mission and ready to seize any opportunity to oppose Bishop Payne, Crummell, in the early 1860s, decided to join ranks with Stokes in fighting for an independent church organization in Liberia.

In 1862, the black clergy, excluding Crummell and Stokes, refused to accept Bishop Payne's proposal for a voluntary mission organization, with him (Payne) having absolute power. Instead, the black clergy requested a full-fledged church. The Board of Missions rejected their request on the ground that the idea of a self-governing Liberian church was premature. Later that year, Crummell joined forces with Stokes and other black clergy in drawing up a response to the charge of "prematurity." Their major contention was that Episcopal laymen in Liberia enjoyed political and civil privileges, and they wanted ecclesiastical rights as well. Bishop Payne promised to present their objections before the October 1862 General Convention, but he never did. In February 1863, the black clergy, Crummell and Stokes included, held a convocation in Monrovia in order to organize "the Protestant Episcopal church in Liberia." Bishop Payne was invited to this convocation, and not only did he enthusiastically endorse the proposals of the convocation, offering but minor reservations, but he promised to fight for the implementation of their requests. However, the bishop misrepresented the proceedings of the convocation to both the Foreign Committee and local teachers and ministers. Crummell's alliance with Stokes in fighting for an independent church caused some of his English

friends alarm. For example, the Reverend John Ketton, an English clergyman whom Crummell when in
England had befriended, wrote to Crummell denouncing Stokes's academic training ("He shouldn't have
been ordained"), and argued that political independence should not necessarily mean ecclesiastical
independence. Appealing to Crummell's intellectual
ambitions, Ketton informed Crummell that Cambridge University was contemplating granting him a
master's degree.[37]

However, in July 1864, an open letter from the
Liberian clergy, signed by Crummell and Stokes
among others, was addressed to the Special Committee on Missions making the most serious charges
against Bishop Payne.[38] They accused him of being a
racist: "He seems to have acted under the impression
that our souls needed the idea of personal inferiority,
as a sort of preparation for our work, in connection
with himself." They further accused him of being a
supporter of slavery, "volunteering defenses of
slavery and slaveholders." Worst of all, they claimed
that he was unjust in his treatment of Liberian
clergymen, preferring to send for foreign
missionaries to serve in their settlements. In bold and
clear language, they protested: "We are tired of all
this ill treatment and think that it ought NOW to
come to an end," and went on to explain in language
that must have been Crummell's: "We came to this
country hoping to find *one* spot on earth, where an
American black man could entertain feelings of self-
respect. . . . It is our right in this land as well, ec-
clesiastically, as politically; and we cannot yield it."
They made it quite clear that they would no longer
meet with Bishop Payne in conventions, synods, or
convocations: "For ten years we have been . . .
struggling and suffering. We can stand it no longer."
They concluded their ringing indictment of Bishop
Payne with a thinly veiled warning that they were
waiting to see if the Episcopal church in America

would support a man whose actions clearly said, "You blacks are nobodies and have no rights; and when you don't suit us we will trample you in the dust, even in your own country."

In his determination to oust Bishop Payne from his post in Liberia, Crummell was willing to collaborate with Eli Stokes, a man for whom he had little respect, in a joint effort to establish a church under the government of black men. Crummell was painfully learning that for black solidarity to be achieved one had to have strange bedfellows. Personal experiences were forcing Crummell to formulate a Pan–African solidarity for the purpose of black independence. This was a significant shift in his Pan–African vision which was wont to see black unity, not as a step towards sovereignty, but as a necessary step toward achieving integration and acceptance within white society. Unfortunately, when his struggles with Bishop Payne ceased, Crummell retreated from his black nationalistic stance to his former black solidarity front in order to demand respect in the eyes of the white world. For the present, however, the angry Episcopal clergyman formed an unholy alliance, in his eyes, with Eli Stokes to wrest control from Bishop Payne.

Bishop Payne did not suffer these attacks with Christian forbearance. First, he appointed the Reverend Alfred F. Russell, a black clergyman who, like Crummell, was once disconnected from the Foreign Mission, head of a congregation that was rightly under Crummell's jurisdiction. Next, in a private letter to the Foreign Committee, he offered a detailed defense against the charges made by the black clergy.[39] Suspecting that Crummell was the one who drew up the letter of indictment, he made his defense a direct attack against Crummell. He represented Crummell as someone who sought power and prestige and who was a poor manager of financial matters. He reminded the Foreign Committee: "While receiving as much salary as any other missionary except the Bishop, he [Crummell] wrote that he could not live on his salary." He pointed out by subtle implications that this man who "could not live on his salary" had built a house in Monrovia, had bought a farm along the St. Paul's River, and had erected a cottage on this farm. He rehearsed all of Crummell's old financial problems with the Trinity church building in Monrovia, his inability to live within his appropriations, and his having to break connection with the Foreign Committee "chiefly on the grounds of the impossibility of keeping his financial matters in a satisfactory state." However, Bishop Payne's major thrust against Crummell seemed to be the pride of this black man. He charged that Crummell "esteemed himself *the proper leader* in all respects for the church and the nation." The bishop's real fear of Crummell had surfaced: Crummell wanted to supplant him as bishop of Liberia. He warned the Foreign Committee that Crummell strongly believed that "the white man has *no rights or mission in Africa.*" The bishop further alleged that it was Crummell's prejudice and hatred against all white missionaries in Africa that had motivated him to organize the black clergy to set up an independent church in Liberia. Even the Reverend Garreston W. Gibson, Bishop Payne reported, who had signed the letter of indictment with Stokes and Crummell, had once stated: "Liberia would have been far better off, if Mr. Crummell had never come to this country."

The bishop's defense confirmed rather than exonerated him from the charge of racism. His report attempted to persuade his fellow white clergymen on the basis of race to check these black clergymen who refused to play second fiddle to the white missionaries sent out by the Foreign Committee. Unfortunately, the Foreign Committee chose to play a game of "wait and see," and took no decisive action against either the bishop or the black clergymen. Bishop

Payne felt encouraged by this inaction on the part of the home office, and in his 1864 Annual Report of the Board of Missions to the Foreign Committee, he made a verbal and published attack against Crummell. He claimed that Crummell was negligent in his work at St. Peter's in Caldwell and that he had established a new church (St. John's) which infringed on the Reverend Alfred Russell's congregation.

Crummell was livid with rage when he read this report, and in a letter to the Foreign Committee, he stated bluntly, "Gentlemen, this representation of me in Bishop Payne's report is a very gross and wicked thing."[40] Crummell went on to give a detailed account of the work he did at St. Peter's, and pointed out that St. John's Church was not new, for he had ministered it from 1856–1858. He had been patiently awaiting this one–to–one opportunity to expose Bishop Payne. Visitors to Liberia and friends in England and America had told him over the twelve years he had worked in Liberia that Bishop Payne had spread negative reports about him. To contradict these reports, Crummell offered to have responsible people attest to the falsity of Bishop Payne's claims, and in a tone of self–righteous indignation he refused to have himself compared with "this Mr. Alfred Russell."[41] It was clear that Bishop Payne was soliciting the support of the mulatto clique which detested Crummell, but he (Crummell) admitted his unpopularity among the Mr. Russells: "I have not, and will not hold my peace concerning the gross evils which exist in the social and domestic life [of the Liberian settlers]."[42] To underscore the irresponsible point of view that Bishop Payne held, Crummell claimed that several responsible people had solicited his services for the government.

One year following Crummell's response to the annual report, Bishop Payne appointed a Mr. Blackledge as rector at St. Peter's. Undoubtedly, the bishop knew of the difficulties Crummell was then having at Liberia College, and he was trying to force the black clergyman to leave the country in frustration. Crummell, however, stood up to the bishop. He attested in no uncertain terms: "I have no intention of leaving this country, and shall not." He proceeded to organize the parishioners of St. Peter's to sign a petition declaring that they wanted the Reverend Alexander Crummell who was elected rector of St. Peter's in 1863 as their rector, and he sent a copy of this petition to Bishop Payne and to the secretary of the Foreign Committee.

It was no easy matter for Crummell to organize his parishioners, for when he first came to Caldwell, he was physically attacked and driven out of his church for preaching against drinking and adultery, and having all the rumshops in the area closed down. However, he eventually had won over the citizens of the community, had built a church, and had established a congregation. They now came to his assistance against Bishop Payne.

In a separate letter to the Foreign Committee, Crummell attacked the immoral character of the man Bishop Payne was appointing over him, and he emphatically declared that no one could ever force him out of Africa: "Who has a better right to emigrate to Africa than I?"[43] He refused to yield his jurisdiction over St. Peter's Church at Caldwell to the Reverend Mr. Russell, but the controversy over the rectorship at St. Peter's dragged on for more than a year.[44] Then, in a letter to the secretary of the Foreign Committee (June 1, 1867), Crummell sought to bring the whole matter surrounding his rectorship at St. Peter's to a head by recapitulating the history of the evolution of St. Peter's, including his election as rector in 1863 and the Reverend Mr. Stokes's death in 1866, and he concluded the letter by claiming that it was his sermon on divorce and his unrelenting attacks on the excesses and immorality of the clergy that had made him so disliked among certain members of his church. The home office responded to Crummell's letter by assigning him to the station at Crozerville which was an undeveloped and semideserted region on the outskirts of the interior. Crummell wrote a letter bewailing the hardships such a transfer would entail—no housing for his family of eight, the higher living expenses coupled with his being disconnected from Liberia College, and the many deaths the settlers in that region had suffered. However, faithful to his vow of obedience, he wrote: "I will submit to the will of the Committee."[45] The home office relented and allowed Crummell to remain at Caldwell. Crummell was stationed at this post in Caldwell until he left Liberia. Bishop Payne had not ceased his harassment of Crummell for he had reported to the secretary of the Foreign Committee that Crummell had accepted a political office. Crummell promptly and somewhat proudly responded that, indeed, he had been offered nominations for chief justice, vice president, and president of Liberia, but he had declined all the offers and Bishop Payne knew it. He openly accused the bishop of being a liar.

The year 1869 turned out to be the lowest point in his conflicts with Bishop Payne. From an unexpected source, the bishop received assistance in his quarrels with Crummell. Sidney, Crummell's son, turned against his father. Deeply hurt by this filial disloyalty, the embittered clergyman complained that "an unnatural assault" was made on him.[46]

Sidney had been Crummell's special cross to bear. The father had sacrificed to have his son educated in England, but when Sidney returned to Liberia in 1864, he fell in with the kind of drinking companions who were particularly distasteful to his austere father. Having obtained some measure of independence and freedom while in England, Sidney refused to submit to his father's autocratic and ascetic way of life. He introduced his sisters to his drinking companions and encouraged them to rebel against their father's way of life. Crummell was, indeed, imposing on his wife and children the kind of severe existence that had best suited his temperament. His eldest daughter actually married one of Sidney's drinking companions, and her mother had approved it. Crummell's family was feeling stifled and inhibited, and Sidney's arrival was welcomed as a breath of fresh air. Feeling his authority being threatened, Crummell drove his son out of his house. Fourteen months later, Sidney, the prodigal son, returned begging forgiveness, and he offered to teach in Crummell's school for no salary. Crummell accepted his son back into the fold and actually tried to get the Foreign Committee to give his son a salaried appointment.[47] However, Sidney fell back into his drinking ways, and everyone, including Crummell's wife, knew about Sidney's drunken habits, but no one told Crummell who was busy tending to his missionary stations in Virginia, New Georgia, and Congo Town. When Crummell found out that his son was not only himself drinking recklessly but had also given the schoolchildren liquor, he was dumbfounded. He summarily dismissed his son and reported to the home office: "I fear he [Sidney] is utterly unreclaimable."[48]

It was then that Sidney wrote his infamous letter denouncing his father and sent it on to Bishop Payne. In the letter, Sidney claimed that his mother and sisters were being persecuted by his father: "My mother is barely clad, my sisters are in the same condition . . . they have not decent food to eat . . . [and are placed] under humble subjection to . . . his supreme authority." He further alleged that his father had not spoken to his mother in over two years and that he had publicly whipped his oldest daughter through the streets of Caldwell. Then, getting to the real reason for the letter, Sidney pointed out that he had taught school for fifteen months and was not given a cent. He concluded his letter with a not totally unrepresentative portrait of Crummell: "The whole of the difficulties in our family is caused by an unforgiving domineering temper which requires servile submission."[49]

In Bishop Payne's hands this letter became a spear to pierce Crummell's heart. The malicious bishop gave the letter to the Reverend Alfred Russell, Crummell's bitterest enemy, and Crummell had to suffer the humiliation of seeing his wife and daughters summoned before a grand jury over the matter of maltreatment and neglect. His wife refused to go, and his eldest daughter went and denied the charges. The jury threw out the indictment, but the damage was done. Crummell's name was scandalized, and he wrote to the home office denying that in his twenty-five years of marriage he had ever struck his wife. The fact is that Sidney had never accused Crummell of striking his wife! Crummell was very bitter with his wife for indulging Sidney's drunken ways, and with Bishop Payne for handing over the letter without consulting Mrs. Crummell or anyone in the family about the allegations. Refusing to bend, Crummell wrote to the secretary of the Foreign Committee, "Bishop Payne has damaged the church, *not me*."[50] In fact, the wounded clergyman was supported by many notable persons including merchants, college professors, clergymen, former President Warner, soon-to-be-President James Roye, and his close friend, Edward Blyden.[51]

When Sidney heard of the hurt his letter had caused his father, he was repentant and wrote letters recanting his accusations concerning a promised salary: "There was no rascality in my father's actions at all; he acted truthfully and justly to me through the whole affair."[52] To Crummell Sidney wrote: "I feel disgraced, humbled, and mortified." It should be noted that Sidney never recanted his allegations against Crummell's treatment of his wife which included placing one of the daughters in charge of the household over the head of Mrs. Crummell. As to the austere living demanded of his family, Crummell defended it by saying: "We are poor people and we have to to live as such."[53] The relationship between Crummell and his wife was obviously strained; Crummell referred to her as being "pertinacious and violent," and she collaborated with Sidney and her daughter who had married one of Sidney's friends unknown to Crummell. The autocratic tendency in Crummell came out when he defended his actions against his daughter's marriage by declaring, "I am head of my family,"[54] and his self-righteousness showed up when he analyzed his persecution in terms of evil bearing down on innocence and goodness: "I have lived free of politics, corruption and rum, but my quietness and seclusion have only exaggerated the dislike of a few bad men."[55] Yet it must be said in Crummell's defense that he was provoked beyond human patience, and like King Lear, he was "a man more sinned against than sinning."

The last mention we have of Bishop Payne in Crummell's correspondence was an apology by Crummell to the home office for the strong language he had used three years earlier in calling the bishop a liar.[56] In his exchanges and disagreements with Payne, Crummell had moved to an independent nationalistic posture, but he had also grown to distrust even more the mulatto element among the American settlers. His hope now turned largely on the native African.

Tension between the American settlers and the native Africans had strained Crummell's Pan-African dream of international unity during his early years in Liberia. His first impressions of West Africa in general, and Liberia in particular, were rosy and optimistic. But a more realistic sentiment about the state of affairs in Liberia came in a personal letter which he had written within a year of his arrival to the secretary of the Foreign Mission, "I cannot write glowing reports of the nation and of the people . . . and yet be a true and honest man."[57] This other Liberia which did not merit "glowing reports" was the Liberia that had a great impact on Crummell's life.

The conditions he met on his arrival in Liberia were unsettling for this Pan-African idealist. There was serious conflict between the Liberian settlers and the native Africans. Conflicts between the Afro-Americans and the native Africans went back to the very founding of Liberia. The 1822 expedition under Eli Ayers and Robert Stockton ran into trouble with the tribes who refused to allow "foreigners" to settle in their land. Only when Jehudi Ashmun arrived (assisted by Lot Carey of the earlier expedition) were the tribes repelled and their land settled by these foreigners.[58] The buying of land by the foreigners from the so-called African chiefs and then the sub-duing of the natives by force was a replay of the European and American Indian conflict. But Crum-mell rationalized two important mitigating circum-stances in the Liberian case. The foreigners were actually African descendants who were returning to the land of their forefathers, a land from which they had been involuntarily taken by force. Crummell, himself, invoked this argument from birthright in defending his decision to settle in Liberia: "I have no intention of leaving this country. . . . I have come back to within a day's journey of the very spot whence my own father was stolen in his boyhood and where my poor ancestors lived from time immemori-al. Who has a better right to emigrate to Africa than I?"[59] An even more important defense on behalf of African colonization was the moral argument that a Liberian settlement could hasten the abolition of the slave trade and of slavery itself. The new settlers in Liberia hoped to develop the coast lands so effec-tively that they would be able to put a stop to the slave traffic which was still being carried on between callous Africans and money-greedy Europeans. Thus, in special cases, the wars against slave-trading native Africans had moral justification. Yet, one has to discriminate between the insensitive, power-hungry native Africans who voluntarily participated in the slave trade, and the masses of Africans who were merely victims of the slave trade, and sought only to live honest lives. Moreover, the settlers saw it as their duty to keep up hostile relations with most of the coastal and inland tribes, and in the very year of Crummell's arrival (1853), the Liberians were actively fighting a war against King Boombo and his Vai people.[60] Edward Blyden, the outstanding Liberian intellectual and politician, who went on this expedition against King Boombo, was so impressed with the king and his Vai kingdom, that he henceforth adopted the policy that the settlers should work closely with the native Africans.[61] Crummell predictably would become a close friend of Blyden and work toward bridging the gap between the settlers and the natives.

This gap was real and destructive, for it separated the Liberians not only from native Africans at large but even from friendly native Africans who lived in the republic. From the very outset, the Liberian settlers separated themselves from the Africans, thinking themselves superior. This attitude of superiority was somehow linked with the "manifest destiny" that New World black people, Crummell included, thought was their role. The only way Christianized black people could justify the ways of God to the black race was by seeing in slavery a way to expose Africans to Christ's teachings. After a period of suffering and bondage, the baptized Ne-groes would return as missionaries to the land of their forefathers and bring civilization in the form of Christianity to the ignorant and backward Africans. Crummell rationalized slavery thus: "It seems a divine law that when God designs a people to perform some single service, to work out some larger and magnificent destiny, he carries them through the dread ordeal of pain, and suffering, and woe. ... Through such a severe training this African race has been passing, during the centuries ... [to give] us a mental and manly preparedness ... for a great work."[62] The great work, Crummell went on to explain, was "the civilizing of Africa."

This posture of superiority of black Americans over native Africans based on Christian enlighten- ment quite naturally flowed over into the political and social life-styles of the Liberian settlers, and, instead of eagerly embracing their fellow Africans with missionary zeal as Crummell had hoped, they systematically excluded the native Africans from participation in the life of the Republic of Liberia. The native Africans were hired as house servants and were considered an inferior class. William Nesbit claimed that there was slavery in Liberia. Nesbit wrote, "I would a thousand times rather be a slave in the United States than in Liberia."[63] Samuel Williams denied Nesbit's claim of slavery in Liberia: "I do most solemnly declare that Nesbit lied in making this assumption."[64] However, Williams did admit to indolence on the part of the colonists who felt that they had to have servants much like the Southern life in America bred.[65] He also noted that native labor was cheaper than American labor and so most of the labor of the nation was done by the native Africans. The evidence suggests that without a doubt the native Africans were being exploited by the New World black people. Indeed, the very constitution of the new Republic of Liberia denied the vote to native Africans and excluded them from citizenship rights.

It grated on Crummell painfully to see his fellow Americans meting out to the Africans the same kind of second-class citizenship that black Americans resented so bitterly in America. In the spirit of Pan- African unity, Crummell, in his first official sermon in Monrovia in 1854, went against the prevailing attitudes of the original settlers by defending the "natural religion" of the native Africans. Without denying the efficacy of Christianity and the need for missionary work in order to bring Christ to the native African, Crummell argued that Africans did have a religion that had worth and value, for it came from God in the form of a natural religion. The idea of God, he insisted, "is the generative principle of the mind's active power and activity."[66] Given that premise, it was absurd to suppose that *any* society is without religion. Religion was deep–seated in the mind of man, even in the minds of non–Christian Africans who were "backward" in the ways of modern living. By driving in this assertion, Crummell was striking a blow for Pan–Africanism. If common ancestry could not persuade the settlers to live in unity and harmony with the native Africans, perhaps the idea of God could serve as the unifying force. The very religion the settlers had thought set them aside from the natives, Crummell used as an instrument for unification. The better he got to know the Africans, the less defensive he became in seeking to justify their acceptance. He began to see them as the hope for Liberia and the central force in his Pan–African movement. Even before Mount Vaughan, while working at a "black settlement" in the interior, he had an opportunity to observe the native African closely, and he was deeply impressed. In his 1855 semiannual report he wrote: "[These Africans are] rather superior to most emigrants: industrious, their patches of ground neat and clean, thrift manifest . . . intelligent in conversation, sober, respectable, and religious."[67] As for the settlers, he complained that "the sweeping whirlwind of both *trading* and *politics* . . . [is carrying] off laymen and ministers almost as soon as they arrive."

While at Mount Vaughan, Crummell established several stations towards the interior, and his missionary work was centered among the native Africans. So firmly established was the prejudice against the native African that even Crummell, whose father was a native African, expressed wonder at the quality of life of the Africans. He actually felt pride in "discovering" that the Africans were intelligent people who lived in a highly organized society. He might have thought that his father and Garnet's father were unique Africans! He wrote to his Afro–American brothers in America that he could attest to the Africans' moral, social, and political integrity, and asserted proudly that the Africans were "our intellectual equals."[68] Well aware of the prejudices and shame about Africa that he once shared with his Afro–American brothers, he was eager to inform them of his "discoveries" about the African. "We do not know our race," he argued, and claimed that the native African was superior to Afro–Americans in areas that were natural and not cultivated.[69] At least Crummell was willing to acknowledge his prejudices and meet the native Africans on equal footing. He went so far as to see the Africans as the ones who had to accept black people from the New World, and he felt his Pan–African dream becoming a reality when he assured Afro–Americans that "our own thoughtful men [among the native Africans] begin to feel the binding tie which joins them . . . with the Negro race all over the globe."[70] It is interesting to note that Crummell had actually bridged the gap between the continents and was living evidence of the Pan–African ideal. In speaking about Afro–Americans, he included himself, "*Our* intellectual equals," and in speaking about the native Africans, he was one with them also, "*Our* own thoughtful men." Crummell was not only preaching the unification of black people; he transcended his own prejudices and lived the Pan–African ideal.

The "binding tie" that this Pan–African missionary felt held the native African and the Afro–American together was blood. He saw all black people as belonging to "the whole Negro family."[71] Central to his Pan-African concept was the unifying force of race as defined by blood, and he believed that neither time nor place could ever entirely erase the strong currents of kindred blood. Somewhere deep in the inner recesses of man was "the deep consciousness of distinctive race."[72] Though he saw race as being distinctive, he did not see it as necessarily a divisive characteristic. Race could bind large groups of people scattered over the earth into one family, and nations could bind different races together into one people. He envisaged a race or a nation as a part of a greater commonwealth of being and vigorously preached, "There is no isolation; no absolute dis-severance of individual nations; for blood and lineage . . . tend to combine nationalities and link them in indissoluble bonds."[73] Thus, the settlers had to look toward the native African, Liberia toward Africa, and Africa toward all the world. It is within this broader perspective that one can properly understand Crummell's Pan-African mission. Pan-Africanism is but a step toward world unity. Unlike Du Bois, Crummell saw no "double consciousness" problem for black people in America. Afro-Americans could acknowledge the fact of kinship with Africans without abandoning their duties as Americans, for he explained that "cosmopolitan views do not necessarily demand a sacrifice of kinship [or] a disregard of race."[74] The obvious practical problem of mixed blood, with which any theory of race must deal, Crummell simply passed over by defining a black person as any "man who has black blood flowing in his veins."[75] This description of the black person was an appeal on behalf of Africa and not a scientific definition. Crummell was urging all people with "African blood" in their veins to claim proudly their kinship with Africa even at the expense of not acknowledging the fact of kinship with another race. With this kind of bias towards Africa, this committed black man hoped that, in part, the regeneration of Africa would be served.

Increasingly Crummell pressed for the integration of Africans and the Liberian settlers. The stiff test for the viability of this integration was the issue of the Congoes.

A problem raging in Liberia during the early 1860s was the matter of recaptured slaves. The debate centered around the issue of whether the "Congoes," as these recaptured slaves from illegal slaving vessels were called, would prove detrimental to the Liberian society or would become "civilized" and be absorbed into the society. At first, President Stephen Benson, who had succeeded J. J. Roberts as president of Liberia, complained about the "dumping" of these liberated slaves in Liberia. However, Alexander Crummell saw that these men were fellow African brothers and needed help, not rejection by the black American settlers in Liberia. Strongly defending the rights and capacities of native Africans, Crummell assured all who would listen that the children of the indigenous Africans were as adept at learning as the families of the settlers, and he spoke from experience as principal of the high school at Cape Palmas during which time he had native children as students. Many of these African students later became well-trained teachers and missionaries. To Crummell, the Congo was simply another indigenous African who had the misfortune to be captured as a slave. Many of these recaptured slaves were sent to Cape Palmas, and so Crummell had the opportunity to observe them firsthand. He was unequivocal in his verdict that recaptured slaves were effectively integrated and absorbed.[76] Basing his argument on his belief that each race has distinctive characteristics, Crummell pointed out that history showed the black man to have an innate capacity to easily adapt to new circumstances. Historically, the black race had not only withstood the onslaught of European imperialism but had effectively assimilated the ideas and customs of its oppressors: "By a kind of instinctive eclecticism [the black man] draws to himself good and advantages from the nature and the society of *that* people . . . to whom he is subjected . . . and assimilates himself to them, their habits, their political state, and their rules of life."[77] This plastic nature of the black man, which had often come under fire from black nationalists who deplored the easy surrendering of black customs and traditions by the black man in favor of western cultural habits, Crummell saw as a God–given talent of the black race. Within this context, the black missionary saw the Congo as a man who would quite easily become a law–abiding citizen of Liberia, learn the English language, and practice the Christian faith as eagerly and devotedly as any other Liberian citizen. In a letter dated September 5, 1861, he underscored his viewpoint on the Congo question by suggesting that the Congoes were "a providential blessing for Liberians."[78] Not only were they easily assimilating Liberian practices, but they were balancing out the lopsided female population of Liberia, and many of the Congo men were inter-marrying with Liberian women. Crummell did inti-mate that more economic aid was needed in order to properly absorb these new citizens, but so pliant and industrious were these Congoes that without a doubt they were a benefit to Liberia.[79] He felt that Liberia could receive as many as twenty thousand recaptives without suffering any negative repercussions.[80]

The issue of the integration of native Africans with the Liberian settlers helped to crystallize Crummell's concept of civilization. The American- and English–trained missionary had come to Africa with the preconceived notion that the "civilized" black people from the New World had to bring the graces of civilization to the "barbaric" African. Pan-African unity simply meant the settlers must teach what they had acquired in America to the native

Africans. However, having had at Mount Vaughan the opportunity to work closely with the native Africans from the interior of Africa, Crummell realized that the African had developed many social and cultural practices that were essential to a Pan–African civilization. True Pan–Africanism meant the modification of the time–honored traditions of the native Africans with the new ideas which the settlers had learned in America. His new Pan–African concept was founded on the dialectical synthesis of the best from the past with the best from the present. Pan–African Christianity, for example, meant the incorporating of the new (as in the Gospel of Christ) into the old (as in the native African traditions). He did consider some African religious practices to be "superstitious" and some aspects of the social customs to be "barbaric," and in these areas he felt that the Christian message could be helpful. But in terms of the African way of life, he clearly stated: "I have never been disappointed in anything moral, social, or political that I have met within this land."[81]

The native Africans had much of substance to bring to a Pan–African unity. They represented the elder sons of the earth, and so their customs and practices were not primitive in the sense of immature, but in the sense of being remnants of the beginnings. Their art and traditions were what was left of a once great civilization. Crummell did not accept the evolutionary theory of history which suggested that the last or most recent stage was always higher than the first or previous stage. To him, it was "a wrong idea to suppose that the first stages of the world were blind and uncultivated; and equally wrong [was] it to suppose that man *advanced* from barbarism to civilization; instead of that he fell from it."[82] Specifically, he identified the acquisitive principle, "the love of trade," as an asset the native African could contribute to a Pan–African union.[83]

Yet, the native African needed assistance. Crummell seemed to believe that there was an inevitable and somewhat predetermined evolution toward the betterment of the human race from its present state. Using the phrase "nature's upward reaching," he suggested that the human race had to be united in order that "the race, in the aggregate, might go forward and upward."[84] Leave the native African isolated and he would be in a state of barbarism. Equally, the New World black man, or white man for that matter, who had only the veneer of western civilization and lacked the traditional roots and customs of his African or white race is no less a barbarian. To reconcile his view that man did not advance from barbarism to civilization with his belief in nature's upward reaching, Crummell saw history moving in cyclical patterns. Evolutionary progress moved in phases; at the end of each phase there is a fall and new gradual evolution upward begins again. But his new upward movement was quickened by the injection of fresh, new thoughts into traditional customs and behavioral patterns. We must remember that this entire evolutionary scheme which moved in cyclical patterns was overseen and directed by the divine will. Thus could Crummell rationalize slavery as part of the divine plan. Africa, once great, fell; through slavery, "this fact of humiliation," Africans were brought into contact with the ideas of the western world; now, it was the duty of these westernized Africans to return to the land of their ancestors and, fortified with their newly acquired western ideas, help to resurrect the greatness that was once Africa's. Even the introduction of the English language into Africa Crummell saw as part of the providential evolutionary scheme, "designed as a means for the introduction of new ideas into the language of a people; or to serve, as the transitional step from low degradation to a higher and nobler civilization."[85] He never clearly explained his view of a cyclical pattern of history. Was man, for example, absurdly trapped on a plateau of repetitive cycles, or does each cycle go further than the previous cycle as nature continually moves upward and forward? He did speak of a "more noble and more glorious" civilization than "as ever before existed" coming into being in Africa. But he never expounded fully on this idea, and we do not know, for example, if this "more noble" civilization referred to previous African civilizations or world civilizations. Whether history oscillated between low and high points, or corkscrewed upward in cyclical gyrations, the fact remains that Crummell felt that he lived at a time when man was on an upward swing, and the black man had a divinely ordained role to play in this upward thrust of mankind. To effectively fulfill his role, the black man must bring western civilization to Africa, not to replace African civilization but to stimulate the rebirth of ancient African civilization.

Our Afro-American Episcopal clergyman had become an internationalist. His Pan-Africanism transcended nationality and rested firmly on race. Black men from America, the West Indies (for there were some West Indian settlers in Liberia), and Africa, both light-and dark-complexioned, had to live as one family. However, for this Pan-African idealist, any meaningful union needed spiritual values as its binding force. As might be expected, the spiritual values cherished by this Episcopal clergyman emanated from his Christian training.

In Crummell's eyes, Christianity was the major civilizing force which had to be introduced to the native Africans. In order for black people, as a group, to hasten their redemption, they had to uplift their spiritual level. As Crummell put it, "A people are as high as their idea of God."[86] Narrow-mindedly, this Episcopal minister believed that the only correct "idea of God" was the Christian idea. For example, when, in the interior of Africa, he came across the Barline People, who displayed great industrial ener-

gies and manufacturing skills—making their own
military and agricultural instruments, cultivating
their own tobacco, weaving their own cloth, preparing their own salt—he still saw the need for the
"civilizing hand" of the Christian missionary among
these highly developed people before the Mohamme-
dan influence, "the most pestilent hindrance to the
gospel," began to spread its corrupting ways.[87] He
earnestly felt that only the Christian gospel with its
message of "Peace on earth, good-will to men" could
eradicate "the rudeness and barbarism of surrounding
heathenism."[88] Not only did the native Africans need
the values of Christianity, but Crummell could not
envision any worthwhile Pan-African movement that
was not firmly founded on the Christian concern for
spiritual man.

Christianity's attention to both the body and the
soul was particularly attractive to this clergyman.
Since he believed that the physical and the spiritual
were merely different facets of a common soul, the
one being the external manifestation of the other, he
knew that religion needed to attend to both. While
stationed at Mount Vaughan, he delivered a sermon at
Harper, Cape Palmas, on the occasion of the laying
of the cornerstone of St. Mark's Hospital. The context of a hospital ideally fitted his constant theme of
relating the physical to the spiritual. A hospital, in
his eyes, was but the secular equivalent of the
church, and the hospitalized sick had to be made to
realize that physical pain was an outward, palpable
form of internal "disease." He accepted as fact that
only Christianity attended urgently to the physical
needs and to the spiritual needs of man: "The religion
of Jesus is the only one which cares for both body and
soul."[89]

Though his Pan-African ideas were firmly
grounded on the spiritual concerns of Christian doctrine, he never forgot the practical concerns of
Jesus. As is evident in his American addresses, he

was ever mindful of the physical condition as a gateway or door, as it were, to the metaphysical state. Consequently, he considered a religion that was oblivious to the practical affairs of day-to-day living to be empty and fruitless. True spiritual experience grew out of the physical. In unmistakable language he warned, "A spirituality . . . which pretends to such loftiness and elevation that it cannot attend to the affairs of the earth . . . is vain and illusory."[90] He was determined not to allow religion to serve as a cumbersome chain around the neck of his Pan-African nation. He explained that Christianity approved of material wealth provided that it was used to do good and to glorify God. He wanted black people to be "ambitious of riches" provided they had "proper aims and purposes."[91] These aims and purposes were the building of a Pan-African nation which would create for all black people a "pathway of science, letters, religion, and civilization." Crummell had no place in his Pan-African scheme for the black man who sought wealth merely for personal aggrandizement: "No greater curse could be entailed upon Africa than the sudden appearance upon her shores of a mighty host of heartless black buccaneers."[92] It is for this reason he insisted that the native African be introduced to navigational skills and shipping vessels which would help him share in Africa's wealth.[93] The native African had to be taught the ways of Christ, and this meant not only concern for his soul, but also care for his body. The true Christian missionary would encourage the native African not only to pray, but to cultivate sugar, coffee, indigo, cinnamon, and cotton. In fact, Crummell blamed the failure of white Christian missionary work in Liberia on the fact that these missionaries did not sufficiently attend to the practical needs of the Africans.[94]

But Crummell never placed the practical above the spiritual. Always the primary concern must be, "saving and sanctifying the sinful souls of men."[95] In the same breath that he emphasized the grave importance of farming and the development of agricultural produce in the building of a nation, he identified the cultivation of men as the national obligation of Liberia to humankind. With words ringing with confidence, he preached, "It is only men who can make a country."[96] However, he was careful to define "men" as he used it. He endorsed Emerson's concept of self-reliance and energy as essentials for men in the task of nation-building, but it was men's soul which he felt had to be cultivated. As he put it, "the largeness of soul—that quick, glad recognition of noble principles—that love of a reverie for fixed and eternal truth."[97] As readily as men must build roads, fight the deadly ants which seemed to swarm all over Liberia, cultivate crops, establish trade, open up industries, even more so must they learn to recognize the "noble principles," the eternal Truth which was the essence of the other world contiguous to this three-dimensional world of phenomena.

Though Crummell felt that "nations like individuals must respect Truth,"[98] he knew that if a nation was to survive the great upward surge of nature, that nation had to adapt itself to the *Zeitgeist* that was pervading all of the Western world. Emerson had correctly identified that the times demanded hardiness and strength; however, Crummell understood that a more highly evolved human would be a compassionate being. Unfortunately, that stage of development was still some decades away, and so, for a young nation to survive, its people had to display self-reliance and toughness of character: "The Christianity of 2,000 years has not educated the world up to consideration for the weak, nor respect for the lowly and feeble. *That* is to be left for a higher stage of human culture and the golden age beyond."[99] It is important to stress Crummell's divergence from Emerson, for whereas Emerson tended to conform to the survival-of-fittest view-point, Crummell saw that compassion from the strong was an even higher rung on the ladder of evolution. This black Christian man saw perfection coming about as a result of unity, not as a result of strength. However, he was pragmatic enough to realize that if black men were to survive the nineteenth century, they had to generate their own energy of survival and not rely on any other nation to understand their plight.

Ironically, while Crummell was busy laying the foundation for an international black family based on balancing the spiritual with the practical, he was unwittingly sowing the seeds of destruction for his own family. His wife had to endure the deadly fever which afflicted her more than any other member of the family. But worse than this insensitivity to his wife's health was Crummell's financial situation. Economic problems were the basic cause of the breakdown in his family life, which ended in a divorce in 1873. Before she had sailed to England, his wife shared with him economic deprivation that literally brought starvation to her and her children. Now, in Liberia, she still had to suffer economic deprivation. And Crummell's money problems were often of his own doing. For example, when he first volunteered to go to Liberia he proposed an unsalaried position for himself. Though the African Mission did appoint him to a salaried position, yet, as late as five months after his arrival in Liberia, he was still unsettled about his freight expenses and about the arrange-ments for receiving his salary.[100] Moreover, before he was even properly settled in Liberia, he took upon himself the building of a church in Monrovia on so grand a scale that Bishop Payne, his religious superior in Liberia, thought the whole venture too extravagant.

To understand Crummell's lack of understanding of financial matters which touched him personally, one has merely to glance through one of his letters in which he bewails the attacks of fever on his children, complains how "very expensive" are the provisions by merchants, and then ends emphatically, "I beg to call your attention to the absolute need of a good church edifice in this town."[101] And this, two months before his letter concerning arrangements for receiving his salary and having his freight expenses paid! Crummell was demanding, not only from his wife but from his children as well, the kind of rigid ascetic life for which he had prepared himself as a teenager with his friend Sidney. His son Sidney, however, would later publicly condemn his father for having his family suffer through such personal deprivations.

At Mount Vaughan, Crummell was free from the financial problems that had plagued him in Monrovia. Though his major efforts were directed toward the native Africans, he wrote an open letter (in 1860) appealing to "Free Colored Men in America" to "Come over and help us." This letter was written and published at the urging of Martin Delany who, on his 1859 visit to Liberia, was so impressed by Crummell's arguments favoring emigration to Liberia that he felt they deserved to be circulated in black America. Perhaps because of this letter, in 1861 Crummell, along with Edward Blyden, was selected by the Liberian government to visit the United States in order to recruit black Americans to come and settle in Liberia. Crummell had the added responsibility of collecting books for the soon-to-be-opened Liberia College.

Crummell's impending return to America after an absence of thirteen years was momentous. When he had left America in the late 1840s, black opinion, including Crummell's, was overwhelmingly and vigorously opposed to emigration to Liberia chiefly because the black community had rejected the motives of the American Colonization Society. However, with the decade of the 1850s, black people had begun to despair of ever being free in America and had begun to consider alternative homelands. Not only did Frederick Douglass consider exploring the possibilities of black emigration to Haiti, but, in 1854, a conference was called by Bishop James T. Holly, (the first black bishop of Haiti), Martin Delany, and others to consider the feasibility of setting up a New World empire for black people in South America or Central America or Haiti. In 1856, a second conference was called, and Edward Blyden's pamphlet, *A Voice from Bleeding Africa*, which appealed to black Americans to consider Liberia as the possible site for their emigration scheme, was read before the body. Then, in 1857, the Supreme Court handed down the infamous Dred Scott decision which ruled that slaves were property and as such had no rights, and not even in a free state was a slave to have a change in his status. The following year, Delany took the lead in calling a third conference which convened in Chatham, Ontario, Canada, and it was decided that the Niger Valley or Haiti should be explored as prospective sites for a wholesale black exodus from America. In the same year, Crummell's closest friend, Henry Highland Garnet, was elected president of the newly founded African Civilization Society whose aim was to set up an African nation in West Africa. The following year, in 1859, Delany was present at Liberia's twelfth annual Independence Day celebration, and John Brown made his courageous but futile blow at slavery in his raid on Harper's Ferry. In short, the decade of the 1850s was a trying time for all black Americans.

Undoubtedly, black Americans were ripe for listening to emigration schemes. However, they resisted the schemes of the American Colonization Society and sought their own emigration arrangements. Martin Delany, for example, who was in the forefront of all emigration efforts, never stopped his attacks on the American Colonization Society, and Garnet's organization, the African Civilization

Society, wisely sought to shift the emphasis from escaping American slavery to developing Africa's growth, and promoted emigration as a civilizing rather than colonizing scheme. The implied thrust of Garnet's society was particularly important, for in seeking to "civilize" Africa the motion was toward the indigenous African rather than toward black Americans setting up a colony. Both Crummell and his companion Blyden realized how opportune the time was for promoting emigration to Liberia. In fact, the decade of the 1850s saw more Afro-American emigrants coming to Liberia than the total number of the previous thirty years![102] But then came the war. Two months before the arrival of Crummell in America, the Civil War between the Confederacy and the Union broke out. Black Americans in general saw this war as the first crack in the oppressive system of slavery and the first stepping-stone in their journey towards full citizenship rights. Frederick Douglass, who had agreed to visit Haiti in order to consider Bishop Holly's emigration plans, canceled his trip. Martin Delany directed his efforts toward recruiting a black army for the Union, and even Henry Highland Garnet and other black leaders urged all black Americans to close ranks behind the Union flag and fight to preserve an America free from slavery.

Undaunted, Crummell landed in America in May of 1861, established contact with the American Colonization Society which had collaborated with the Liberian government in this recruitment effort, and proceeded at once to address various state branches of this society. *The African Repository*, the literary organ of the American Colonization Society, introduced Crummell to its readers as an author "of pure African blood [who] . . . with his scholarship and learning has consecrated his abilities to the interest of Liberia, and through her to the population of Africa."[103] It is important to note how his racial purity and his concern for all of Africa were given special mention. The Pan-African bias of Crummell was no secret to the people of that age. In America, his attitude toward emigration became widely known through the publication of extracts of his letter "The Relations and Duties of the Free Colored Men in America to Africa" in the April 1861 edition of *The African Repository*. As a matter of fact, the address Crummell made before his various American audiences were mere elaborations of the ideas he had developed in his 1860 letter. Thus the arguments of this letter can be examined as part of his recruitment drive in America.

African emigration was a ticklish question and Crummell knew it. He emphasized in his letter, "I am not putting in a plea for colonization."[104] In fact, he eagerly acknowledged that black Americans had a just claim to reside in America: "Three centuries residence in a country seems clearly to give any people a right to their nationality therein without disturbance."[105] He well understood their rights: "I, too, am an American black man."[106]

But Crummell was determined to have black Americans retain their Pan-African link with Africa. In a May 15, 1861 address, "The English Language in Liberia,"* he reminded his black brothers, "We are [African] by blood and constitution," and even though he personally could confidently say, "My *maternal* ancestors have trod American soil . . . as long as any descendants of the early settlers of [New York]," yet throughout his life he considered himself an African.[107] On more than one occasion in his letter he pointed out, "This is our Africa."[108]

He tackled the emigration issue from three angles. In the first place, he argued in his letter that he did not encourage a wholesale return of black

---

*First given in Cape Palmas in 1860.

Americans to Africa. Like Marcus Garvey who would follow in his footsteps about fifty years later, Crummell sought selective personnel to build up his Pan-African nation, men "who are anxious for the welfare of the whole Negro family."[109] He repeated this plea for selective emigration before the New York State Colonization Society on May 9, 1861: "Africa has a . . . need for *civilized emigrants*"[110] (his emphasis).

His second approach to emigration was to tie it in with commercial enterprise. Black Americans should consider emigrating to Africa in order to make money. He openly declared that the resources of Africa were God's gift to the Negro race, and he urged black Americans to invest their "dead and unproductive" capital in Liberian enterprises. The question was not colonization, but whether Europeans or African descendants would cultivate the wealth of Africa. Africa had the most productive lands in the world and merely needed skill and enterprise "to raise her." Black Americans could form corporations and companies for investment purposes, set up trading posts along the African coast to trade in nuts, dyes, gums, fruits, vegetables, tobacco, cotton, and so forth. With their navigational skills and shipping vessels, black Americans could share in Africa's wealth. He felt that if black people chose not to develop the riches of Africa, then it was not only permissible, but divinely ordained, that white people should![111] Crummell kept stressing in his letter that this commercial enterprise had no necessary connection with emigration or colonization: "On *this* platform [commercial enterprise], Douglass and Delany [who represented the two extreme sides on the issue of colonization] can stand beside the foremost citizens and merchants of Liberia."[112] He reiterated this appeal to recognize the economic opportunity in Liberia in almost all his addresses in America. For example, before the Massachusetts Colonization Society on May 29, 1861,[113] Crummell remarked on the vast strides Liberia had made during his eight years' residence in the young nation. Crops like coffee, sugar, and cotton were being profitably cultivated; gold, ivory, and palm oil were fast becoming important exports; shipbuilding and ship-ownership were thriving investments, and, most importantly, exports were exceeding imports—always a healthy sign in a nation's economy. Even while advertising these incentives for emigrating to Liberia, he drew loud applause from his audience as he struck out against the American stereotyping of the black man as being traditionally lazy: "Give the Negro some incentive to labor, and there is not a more plodding or industrious man in the world than the African."[114]

The third approach Crummell brought to the emigration issue was based on racial responsibility. Africa, he argued, was in a wretched condition, "wasting away beneath the accretions of civil and moral miseries."[115] The very language of the African, Crummell ignorantly felt, needed to be "civilized."[116] But this state of desolation and ruin was a temporary condition, and he earnestly sought to convince his American listeners that "Ethiopia" was on the verge of stretching forth her hands once more.[117] He believed that God had great designs for Africa which lay there as a great black egg waiting to be hatched: "Africa remains in peace, and stands waiting,"[118] he assured his audience in Massachusetts, and he carried this message of hope to audiences in New York, Boston, and other northern cities. On June 2, 1861, he addressed an all-black audience. He argued that the present time was the time for black people to cash in on all the hurt and pain the race had endured. Throughout his lecture tour of the United States, he repeated his interpretation of the "fortunate fall" of the black man. Through the agency of slavery, black men received the severe training that any people must endure in preparation for a great work. It was the responsibility, therefore, of former slaves and descendants of slaves to return to Africa and undertake the great work of Africa's redemption. Drawing on the mystical laws of God, he enunciated the law of compensation: "God lifts up men from lowly degradation to evangelize the great continent of Africa."[119] It was not a new message, but he hoped that by adding the incentive of economic opportunity to the oft repeated rationalization of slavery as a preordained phase of "preparation," he would be able to persuade the "proper" kind of Afro-American "to join us in Africa, for the regeneration of that continent."[120]

A major consideration on the matter of Liberian emigration was the growing interest among black Americans in Haitian emigration. Bishop Holly was writing a column in the *Weekly Anglo-African* concerning the success of colored Americans who had emigrated to Haiti. In the April 27, 1861 issue of this black newspaper, almost all of page four was devoted to "Haitian advertisements." At a testimonial ceremony for his best friend, Henry Highland Garnet, Crummell broached the issue of Liberia versus Haiti. The strategy of Crummell's appeal on behalf of Liberia was to dispel from the minds of his black audience the feeling that the native African was inferior.[121] As to the question of the particular region for settlement in Africa, Crummell, in his "Relations and Duties of Free Colored Men," had already pointed out that the divine design, to which he seemed to have a special hot-line, had set aside Central Africa, which Delany and his followers favored, for the free and cultivated men of Sierra Leone.[122] Liberia, then, should be the Africa to which Afro-Americans should gravitate. The American Colonization Society might have its own reasons for wanting black Americans to colonize Liberia, but black people should come, guided by the design of God. When Garnet responded at the testimonial, he declared compatibility between the Haitian and Liberian ventures by stating his life's motto to include: "African Civilization; [and] Haitian Emigration." In other words, black Americans could be invited to live as citizens in Haiti, but Africa must be approached as a country needing help in the matter of civilization.

Not only had Crummell to contend with Haitian emigration, he also had to deal with the problem of Irish immigrants in America. The *Anglo-African* kept a close watch on these foreign refugees who were being preferred to native black Americans. Irish immigrants were entering the United States in 1861 at the rate of 2,377 a day![123] Black Americans were determined not to surrender their citizenship rights to this influx of European immigrants, and so any suggestion of returning to Africa as the American Colonization Society proposed was completely rejected. Crummell, as his 1860 "Letter to the Colored Americans" explained, was sympathetic to the plight of black Americans, and based his back-to-Africa appeal on grounds of evangelization and civilization. He did not neglect the profit-making motive, and before black audiences, he dissociated his efforts from those of the American Colonization Society.

The spirit of Pan-African unity was the underlying appeal of Crummell's entire recruitment effort. He appealed to black Americans to look beyond where they lived to continental Africa. "Let our godliness exhale like the odor of flowers," he urged, and then with passionate love he would stress, "This is our Africa." Significantly, he observed that the Liberian nation was composed of a cross section of black people from the West Indies, America, and continental Africa.[124] He warned his Afro-American brothers that they must first live for the good of their kind and "then for the world."[125] Couched in the warning was the essence of Crummell's

Pan-African goal. First, black people must attend to their own needs *as a group; then*, they should work towards a world unity. Pan-Africanism was a stage or phase in a larger movement toward the establishment of one human family. Within this context, he could see the English language as a tool for unifying black people among themselves and with the outside world.[126] Only in this Pan-African sense can there be any sense to Crummell's claim that Christ intended English to be the language of West Africa.[127]

An important advance that Crummell expressed in his Pan-African concept was the central role of women in the building of the Pan-African nation. He condemned "the general frivolousness of the female mind" and felt that it was time for the world to do justice to the intellect of women. Breaking away from the common practice of the times, he urged his fellow black brothers and sisters "to raise our daughters and sisters to become the true and equal companions of men and not their victims."[128] Cognizant of the fact that the mental inferiority of women would retard the progress of children and young people in general, he recommended as a "master need," the establishment of "a FEMALE SEMINARY of high order, for the education of girls."[129] This demand for the academic training of women in as regular and routine a manner as men enjoyed was truly a revolutionary demand on Crummell's part. Throughout his life, he extolled the remarkable role of women, and of mothers in particular, in the shaping of the lives and characters of all men, great and small alike. Later in his life, he offered an insightful address on "Black Women of the South," in which he predicted that the hope of the black race in America lay in the cultivation of the ex-slave woman and her female descendants. In Liberia, he saw an excellent opportunity for a young nation to set an example to the world by "raising the standard of female education."[130] As we would have the woman beautiful, attractive, and moral, so should we have her dignified and intellectual.

Generally speaking, Crummell made a favorable impression on the black community during his American trip even if his recruitment drive did not produce many emigrants. In addition to his lecture tour, he was successful in collecting books for Liberia College. The new president of the college, Mr. J. J. Roberts, publicly thanked Crummell for his job of collecting books for the college, and in the inaugural address on January 23, 1862, at the formal opening of the Liberia College, President Roberts acknowledged that "Through the exertions of Professor Crummell . . . a number of valuable books have been obtained . . . to form the nucleus of . . . an extensive college library."[131]

In 1862, Crummell and Blyden were again commissioned by the Liberian government to return to America and continue their recruiting efforts. The American Colonization Society had realized that not only were American blacks despairing about ever being fully integrated into American society after the harrowing experiences of the 1850s, but now the United States government, including President Abraham Lincoln, was seeking a solution to the race problem in America, and Lincoln was partial to colonization. In 1862, before a black American delegation, Lincoln had said, "Not a single man of your race is made the equal of a single man of ours."[132] Moreover, on Crummell's visit to America, so anxious was Lincoln to promote the colonization idea that a Boston newspaper had Lincoln attributing to Crummell statements concerning the forced emigration of blacks, statements which Crummell had never made. As a result, Lincoln, in a letter to Crummell, had to retreat: "Neither you nor anyone else have [sic] ever advocated . . . the compulsory transportation of freed slaves to Liberia, or elsewhere."[133] Despite the Civil War which was raging on, black Americans were still despised and unwanted, and Liberia had hoped to make the prejudices of white America her gain. The American Colonization Society anticipated much success in the recruiting efforts by Crummell and Blyden, and the corresponding secretary of the society assured Crummell in a letter, "I cannot doubt that precious fruits will spring up from your labors during your visit to the United States."[134] One of Crummell's greatest catches was the great African missionary, Bishop Henry M. Turner, who wrote that it was an address by Alexander Crummell that made him a convert to African repatriation.[135] The address to which Turner referred was probably one Crummell delivered before the Annual Conference of the AME Church held in Baltimore in August 1862.

The *Anglo-African*'s notice of Crummell's return to recruit in 1862 read: "This movement [to recruit] will be entirely distinct from that of the Colonization Society."[136] The society's *African Repository* did give poor coverage of Crummell's activities during his 1862 visit to America. Yet the claim that the American Colonization Society had nothing to do with the recruitment efforts of Crummell and his fellow Liberian commissioners was obviously not true. It was noted that the executive body of the American Colonization Society had resolved to aid these Liberian commissioners' efforts by offering to all who wished to migrate to Liberia free passage, six months' support after arrival, and the usual funds allotted to immigrants.[137] Furthermore, the New York Colonization Society agreed to pay Blyden's salary as professor at Liberia College.[138] Dissociation of Liberian recruitment policies from American colonization schemes was being delicately managed. White America's involvement in Liberia's development was needed. Moreover, the American government displayed goodwill by signing on April 7,

1862, the Abolition of the African Slave Trade Treaty with the United Kingdom. In July of the same year, America formally recognized the independence of Haiti and Liberia. All in all, 1862 augured well for Crummell's dream of Liberia's becoming the catalytic agent for propelling Pan-African unity among black people all over the world.

On his return to Liberia after his United States trip, Crummell took up his position as professor of philosophy at Liberia College. Thereafter followed the lowest period in his sojourn in Liberia. While at Liberia College, he became deeply involved in the mulatto-black conflict. The issue proved to be the final undoing of Crummell in Liberia.

When Crummell first came to Liberia, he had noted that the crack in the Pan-African ideal extended beyond hostility and separation between the native Africans and the Liberian settlers. Among the Liberians themselves there was serious division. The problem of caste, imported from the New World, was ever present. The mulatto class was assuming superior positions in the new republic, and pure black Afro-Americans, as Crummell was, were resenting their treatment. The first president, J. J. Roberts, was so white-looking that a white woman missionary observed in her private diary: "He seemed like an English gentleman but for traces of curliness in his hair."[139] This color question, a major stumbling block in the Pan-African ideal, was closely inter-linked with the settler-native conflict, for the settlers who most resented the native Africans were the mulattoes, who held power in the new nation. In fact, the settler-native problem could be subsumed, for analytical reasons, under the designation of mulatto problem. It is true that no evidence exists that the black settlers resisted the articles in the constitution that excluded citizenship rights to native Africans, and from all reports, no one singled out mulattoes, as distinct from the black settlers, as being the exploiters of black labor. Yet, when Crummell reported that native Africans were intermarrying with the settlers,[140] given the mulattoes' concern for color, it is reasonable to assume that the intermarriage was between black settler and native African. Moreover, when in later years Crummell was reporting on the mulatto effort to retain political power in Liberia, he represented the mulattoes as being particularly brutal towards the native Africans: "The natives they despise and keep down and in these times shoot down with impunity."[141] More than any other single cause, the mulatto problem would prove to be the final undoing of Crummell in Liberia, and, after he had returned to America, having tried for twenty years to make Liberia a truly free and Christian Pan–African nation, he wrote regretfully, "The mulattoes in Liberia will prevent that republic from becoming the great nation it can be."

The mulatto problem came to a head over the establishment of Liberia College. In 1851, an act was passed in the Liberian legislature formally incorporating Liberia College and appointing a board of trustees.[142] However, it was not until January 23, 1862, that the college was formally inaugurated.[143] The chief reason for the delay was the matter of a site. The mulatto Liberian settlers wanted the college established within easy reach of Monrovia; the black Liberian settlers, among whom were Crummell and his good friend Blyden, wanted the college built inland so that native Africans could have easy access to it.[144] Crummell realized that the mulattoes not only separated themselves from the black American settlers but also resented them, and sought to exclude them and the native African in the development of Liberia. As a Pan–Africanist, he opted to join with the native Africans and to resist the mulatto pretenders. However, supported by the New York Colonization Society which had set up a special fund to help with Liberia College, the mulatto faction had their way and the college was established on the coast on the southwest slope of Cape Mesurado, facing the Atlantic Ocean and within the corporate limits of Monrovia.[145] The symbolic significance of this site is important: the college looked back to America rather than forward to the interior of Africa. The mulattoes were clinging to their Eurporean-American ancestry rather than their black African heritage. This attitude went against Crummell's Pan-African mission, and he saw Liberia College as a challenge that would either make him or break him.

In July 1856, J. J. Roberts, having previously stepped down as president of Liberia, accepted the post as president of Liberia College.[146] By January 1858, the cornerstone was laid,[147] and on August 18, 1861, three professors for the college were appointed: the Reverend Alexander Crummell, Edward Blyden, and J. J. Roberts.[148] Of the three professors, Crummell was the only one with an academic degree, and he was appointed professor of intellectual and moral philosophy and of English language and literature. On a temporary basis, he was also to give instruction in logic, rhetoric, and history.[149]

After the confident optimism in Liberia's future that he had expressed while in America, there followed in a matter of four years an uncharacteristic letter of despair from Crummell to the American Colonization Society's Secretary Coppinger: "It is the saddest of all things to come here to Africa, and find one's black face a disgrace both in his ecclesiastical and social relations with half-caste people. For this, after all, is our difficulty; and has been the difficulty for years."[150] The occasion for the surfacing of this underlying friction between the black and mulatto citizens of Liberia was Liberia College. As was previously noted, Crummell and Blyden had favored a more inland site for the college in order to allow easier access to it for the native population. The mulatto faction had won that battle. Now the executive committee of the college headed by President Roberts opposed any programs proposed by Crummell and Blyden to benefit indigenous Africans and advance the black race. Crummell and Blyden wrote "intemperate" resolutions in opposition to the executive committee,[151] and it was alleged that they (Crummell and Blyden) were repeatedly absent from classes and refused to give adequate explanations.[152] According to Blyden, in 1866 Crummell suggested to the trustees of donations "the removal of President Roberts from the Presidency of the College or his own resignation, [and] his resignation was accepted."[153] Blyden detested the hasty manner in which Crummell was removed "without giving an opportunity for conciliation of differences or reconsiderations of any hasty proceedings in Liberia."[154]

Within three months, Crummell's position was filled by Hilary R. W. Johnson who two years later also had to resign.[155] Undoubtedly, the dismissal of Crummell was a loss to higher education in Liberia. Certainly no black institution in the mid–nineteenth century anywhere in the world, let alone Liberia, could afford to dismiss so casually the services of so well–educated, intelligent, and devoted a black man as Alexander Crummell. His goal was simply to help uplift the black race, primarily by educating the black youth. In 1864, he founded in Monrovia the Athenaeum Club, which was very similar to one he had helped to form as a young boy in America, in order to stimulate intellectual discussions and debates and lectures. However, Roberts and his mulatto friends were determined to make education the privilege of mostly light–skinned Negroes and sought to exclude indigenous blacks from all citizen rights. Crummell had reported to Coppinger in March, 1864, "Never have I in all my life seen such bitterness, hate and malice displayed as has been exhibited by the two factions of the state."[156] Blyden openly accused President Roberts of refusing to admit black youths into the college while providing aid to mulatto youths who wished to further their education. Later, Crummell too charged that "it is impossible for a black man of standing to live any longer in Liberia."[157] He joined with the other black professors in trying to get a bill passed in the Liberian legislature that would protect them against the vengeful acts of President Roberts and his mulatto colleagues, but to no avail. There is an April 14, 1866 letter from Blyden to Crummell urging Crummell to fight "the confounded bastards" and to get the trustees in America to take over management of the college, since the bill to modify the power of the executive committee had failed.[158] The result of all this hostility was the dismissal of Crummell in 1866.

The dismissal from Liberia College and the ongoing struggle with Bishop Payne had deeply affected Crummell, and there was fear that he might want to abandon his Liberian dream to build a Pan–African nation. There had been rumors during Crummell's 1862 visit to America that he had been invited to stay on as pastor of St. Phillip's Church in New York City,[159] and now that he had been so callously dismissed from Liberia College, there might have been suspicions that he would indeed return to the United States. Actually, Crummell had visited America in the late part of 1865, probably because of his wife's failing health,[160] and he had brought his mother back with him to Liberia.[161] During these years of the mid–1860s, the thoughts and concerns in letters to Crummell did suggest that he was contemplating leaving Liberia. The Reverend Ketton, for example, wrote to Crummell condemning the Jamaican rebellion,[162] lamenting the deplorable conditions in Haiti, and appealing in language aimed at

Crummell, "Much now depends on Liberia."[163] The letter seemed directed at Crummell's thoughts of leaving Liberia when the nation most urgently needed him. An American correspondent, the Reverend William Tracy, wrote Crummell a sympathetic letter condemning the mulatto versus native African conflict, and promising to bring the matter of the education of Crummell's daughters in an American university before the board of the Foreign Mission.[164] Again, the tone of the letter suggested support and sympathy, to encourage Crummell not to leave Liberia. From Lincoln University, Pennsylvania, a professor wrote to Crummell lauding his work as a teacher in Africa.[165] The sentiments implied someone was about to leave who needed to stay on and continue his good work. Quite clearly, there was a feeling in the air that Crummell was considering a return to America.

The truth is, Crummell was not yet ready to give up on Liberia. In October 1867, he wrote to William Coppinger, secretary of the American Colonization Society, in hopeful language concerning Liberia. He acknowledged that there was "quite steady progress" in agriculture, as well as an "increased self-reliance" in the people. Whatever was lacking in enterprise among the settlers he attributed to the ignorance of the masses, and urgently recommended "forty Free Schools with *good* teachers." He also addressed the concerns about his leaving Liberia. He stated adamantly, "I have had no idea of leaving Liberia." However, he did make reference to a "small unprincipled oligarchy" who might drive him and others out.

Proud of his African heritage, he was determined to stay in Liberia, but he wanted a new Liberia. In another letter to Coppinger dated October 30, 1867, he acknowledged that Liberia needed whatever aid it could receive from whatever quarter, but he insisted, "I do not wish our country to become a colony of any nation." He begged for clothing for the students in his missionary school to which he had returned after his dismissal from Liberia College, but he was firm on the question of Liberia's independence, "having secured independence we cannot give it up."[166] Yet, in the other October letter he had lamented, "The African republic is dead."[167] What he sought for Liberia was the advantage of being an American colony but having the status of a protectorate, "say for twenty-five or fifty years," with specific aid for building roads, setting up model farms, "establishing Manual Labor Schools, in setting up colonies in the interior, and in providing naval guardianship."[168] The reality of practical affairs was sinking into Crummell's consciousness, and though he never abandoned his Pan-African ideal, he now realized that help from white America was essential for the survival of Liberia.

He persisted in his Liberian dream for as long as he could, but he finally broke down. He continued his missionary life, preaching three or four times a week, preparing men for the ministry, holding Bible conferences, and traveling into the Congo to spread God's word. Of these activities at St. Peter's in Caldwell the dedicated missionary wrote, "I feel blessed in my labors."[169] Among those he was preparing for the ministry was his own son, and he happily reported that he had "a very good school under my son's instruction."[170] However, in spite of the brave spirit which he presented, some concern did creep into his letters. He noted that since the end of the American Civil War, there was "no flood of emigrants," but he rationalized, "the descendants of exiles rarely desire to return to the land of their fathers."[171] This last expressed sentiment was a complete about-face from the providential role he had in earlier times seen destined for black Americans.

In addition to this sense of loss about Liberia, personal grief struck. In April 1868, his mother died, and in a June 10 letter to the secretary of the Foreign Mission, he solemnly wrote, "When death comes to [our parents] it leaves a sadness and a suffering which only the grace of God can assuage."[172] By October of that same year, Crummell broke down: "I am a sick man." He complained that Liberia College would not pay him "a farthing" of his salary due and that "worry and anxiety and want [had] knocked me up." His doctor had forbidden any mental work, not even reading, and he lamented the fact, "I cannot do the work I did three years ago." Then this De Profundis letter hit its lowest depths, as he, who only a year before had asserted his determination never to leave Liberia, now confessed that he would leave Liberia but for his duties and embarrassments. Like a defeated and tragic Macbeth he wrote, "I am tied to the spot, and cannot get away."[173] This letter marked the turning point in the Liberian phase of Crummell's life. The Liberia College debacle was having a delayed effect. His health was failing, and he entrusted his life to God, ready to die knowing that he had helped "to advance the Kingdom of Heaven among the rude peoples of Africa."[174] Faced with failure in his earthly mission, Crummell turned to his interior life and consoled himself that "the other life will be ecstatic." Now as in those mystical moments he had experienced as a young man at Oneida Institute, the pious clergyman felt once again with intense passion "the warm desire of heaven."[175] In his 1868 annual report, he summarized the year thus: "The past year has been one of much trial and sickness and death, of hard labor."[176]

Despite the personal hardship and pain, and in the midst of his troubles with Sidney, Crummell kept working in 1869 for a better Liberia. He lamented the destructive force that the mulatto community represented. In a letter dated June 16, 1869, he lambasted the mulatto community for its narrow-minded provincialism and inability to appreciate men like Blyden, Freeman, and Johnson, and he appealed to the American Colonization Society to send "fresh blood and strong brains" for "anarchy or monarchy [was threatening to] burst forth among us." And still filled with optimism he penned, "I want to see free institutions perpetuated here." Isolated as he was then at Cape Palmas, he looked forward to visits to Monrovia to share in fine conversation with Blyden and others, and he moaned how he had to "live on the strength of such conversations for a month."[177] Living on such a meager intellectual diet, it was no wonder that he wrote such words of despair in his De Profundis letter. But even his close friendship with Blyden, perhaps his only solid link with a civilized mind, was to be broken in a matter of two years.

In 1870, he returned to his missionary work. Toward the end of 1869 he had reported that the state of the mission was "unusually favorable," and he requested more "colored" American clergymen to take over some of his stations. He deplored the "noise, hysteria, shrieking" which the Methodist ministers were encouraging, and he prided himself on the fact that his schools were teaching Liberian children to read and write, and the young people to want to work to earn money and to dress properly. A particular mission which he had expanded during the past five years was the training of the Congoes who were being rescued in increasing numbers from illegal slave-trading vessels and were being set free to live in Liberia. He kept up a steady report on the conversion and training of these Congoes. As he moved closer and closer to the indigenous native African, he resisted any mulatto effort to control the Liberian church. On February 1, 1870, he wrote a private letter to the secretary of the Foreign Mission, apprising him of a movement among laymen at Trinity Church in Monrovia to incorporation.[178] It was only after Crummell had left Liberia that the church was formally incorporated, on January 17, 1873.

In secular affairs, things looked up briefly. In 1870, James Roye, a black man of unmixed race, was elected president of Liberia. This ousting of mulatto power raised hopes for men like Crummell and Blyden, but these hopes were short-lived. The mulatto faction did not accept Roye's presidency without contest, and they challenged the four-year term of Roye's office. A referendum held in 1869 voted for a four-year term, but the mulattoes who had a majority in the Senate refused to have the constitution amended. What followed was a political tug-of-war between the blacks and mulattoes, and the outcome of the controversy was the return of J. J. Roberts to political life. In 1871, Roberts was once again declared president of Liberia, and Roye had to flee for his life.[179]

Before the demise of Roye, Blyden himself was slanderously attacked as an adulterer and was barely saved from being lynched by a mob of blacks. He then fled to Sierra Leone.[180] It appears that Crummell, with his scrupulous insistence on moral righteousness, could not accept even the *possibility* of adulterous behavior on Blyden's part and deserted Blyden in his hour of need. Blyden felt betrayed by Crummell, and the fact that his closest friend should join forces with his enemies hurt him deeply:

The sorest trial I have had to undergo is that Reverend Mr. Crummell with whom I labored and fought side by side in Liberia College . . . a man who[m] . . . I defended and assisted . . . on a visit to this colony [Sierra Leone], should so far have allowed himself to be influenced by feelings of envy as to give currency to the malicious reports of our common enemies, and thus make an unfavorable impression upon the mind of the Bishop [Henry Cheetham] respecting myself . . . Et tu, Brute.[181]

In the succeeding years, Blyden kept up this attack on Crummell, accusing him of defecting to the side of the mulattoes. In 1879 Blyden wrote, "I venture to say even now [seven years following Crummell's return to America], in Washington, Crummell is afraid to say that mulatto influence drove him from Liberia,"[182] and in 1880, now fully exonerated from the charge of adultery[183] and the appointed president of Liberia College, he chortled: "I wonder what will Dr. Crummell now think of his despairing position when he left the coast in 1872 saying that Robert's clique would never in this generation be overcome."[184] However, in Crummell's defense against the charge that he capitulated to the mulattoes, it must be noted that the whole ugly business of Blyden's alleged misconduct was centered around blacks. It was with the black President Roye's black wife that Blyden was accused of committing adultery, and it was a mob of black people who dragged Blyden through the streets of Monrovia with the intention of lynching him.[185] Furthermore, if anyone showed collaboration with the mulattoes, it was Blyden who was once married to a mulatto.

A brief assessment of Crummell's behavior towards Blyden and other blacks is proper at this point. It seems clear that Crummell's disapproval of Blyden's actions which were enough to arouse suspicion was not based on envy or malice on Crummell's part. Martin Freeman, a former colleague of both Crummell and Blyden, assessed the situation in a letter to Blyden thus: "I am very sorry Rev. Crummell has treated you so badly, but I hope you will impute it to his foolish ambition to be the greatest Negro in West Africa, and not to malice *per se*. Do not retaliate. He has not injured you, do not injure him."[186] Professor Freeman clearly denied malice on Crummell's part and pointed out that there was no direct injury caused to Blyden by Crummell's behavior. When he blamed Crummell's action on "his foolish ambition to be the greatest Negro in West Africa," Professor Freeman was probably referring to Crummell's striving for a morally perfect life, "greatest" meaning "most saintly." Crummell might not have been without ambition, but it was an ambition that sought to make his life a model for younger black people. Moreover, whenever he became negatively critical or impatient with black leadership, it was always done in personal letters and was focused on improper behavior. For example, in a letter to J. E. Bruce (1895), he wrote about Bishop Turner whom he had converted to African missionary work: "I am glad of [Blyden's] thrust into the ribs of that turbulent, screeching and screaming creature [Bishop Turner]."[187] Or again, when he observed the life-styles of the black bourgeoisie in America, he brushed aside these black fops as "fools . . . who imitate the style and fashion of the Fifth Avenue millionaires."[188] Always he lamented loose living: "I can't say that I see any amendment of morals among our people," and he went on to condemn the scandals at revival meetings and the woeful neglect of the salvation of souls.[189] On the other hand, Crummell was lavish in his praise of men like Garnet, Bishop Holly (who promoted Haitian as opposed to Liberian emigration), and Blyden himself. In fact, he wrote an introduction to Blyden's *Vindication of the African Race*, and though a Freetown publication editorial attacked his bombastic style, it noted the generous attitude of Crummell toward the black leaders in Liberia: "In speaking of the leading man of Liberia he [Crummell] has fallen into that strain of exaggeration, which renders so many Liberians' productions ridiculous."[190] Thus, a more accurate assessment of Crummell during his final years in Liberia came, not from the biting pen of a bitter Blyden, but from the Freetown editorial: "Mr. Crummell, we believe, is a very excellent and philanthropic gentleman."[191] It must be said to Blyden's

credit that as president of Liberia, in 1882, he con-
ferred on Crummell the degree of Doctor of Laws.
Crummell had recognized in early 1871 that the
steps being taken by the Liberian government to oust
President Roye from office would lead to a "bloody
revolution."[192] He thought that by the clergy's
keeping clear of politics he would survive the crisis.
However, he ended up personally embroiled in the
political furor. In August 1871, he went to Sierra
Leone to see about his health, and writing to the
secretary of the Foreign Mission about the state of
political affairs in Liberia, he reiterated: "I am
carefully abstaining from all participation."[193]
Later, back in Liberia, he requested that his letters
be kept private "for no one's life in Liberia is
safe."[194]

The year 1872 began with Crummell once more in
deep financial trouble. He wrote a letter urgently
requesting financial assistance, but was upbraided for
violating "the rules of missionary" by not sending his
financial accounts for 1870 and 1871. He promptly
apologized for his negligence, blaming his inadver-
tence on the deteriorating state of his health, and
sent to the home office fully itemized accounts for
the two years in question, drafts included. Together
with his deteriorating health and his financial
difficulties, the political turmoil reached his own
home. With the accession of Roye to the presidency,
Crummell's son, Sidney, returned to Liberia from
Sierra Leone and became the acting secretary of
state. However, he became involved in the political
uprising and was shot at while trying to warn President Roye of assassins. The upshot was that Sidney
was arrested and sent to prison for two and a half
years. This imprisonment of his own son, who Crummell reported behaved in "an exemplary manner,"
impelled Crummell to write a detailed account of the
state of affairs in Liberia as he saw it. Innocent
people were being hanged and imprisoned, and the

streets were unsafe for all citizens. He identified the source of this state of confusion as the mulattoes, "a whole class of persons, who are opposed to culture, improvement, and native elevation." He pointed out that these men had always been against Liberia College and had formally declared: "We don't want any of these educated men here!" He himself was threatened with "a bullet through my head." For the first time in his life, Crummell reported that Liberia was on the brink of total collapse: "A whole country is going to ruin." In utter disgust, he declared: "You cannot save the Americo–Liberian population!" They lacked vitality, their families were becoming extinct, and all their villages were being covered by bush. Among the American element there were more deaths than births, emigration from America had rapidly decreased, and the native Africans, offended by their treatment at the hands of the American settlers, were taking over the country. With a last desperate plea, Crummell appealed, "If the American government does not take us in hand, we shall have to seek the protective governance of England."[195] His report was a total indictment of the rulers in Liberia. He felt that unless drastic changes were made in Liberia, the entire missionary effort would have been wasted.[196] The practical affairs of state had moved Crummell a long way from his doctrine of "manifest destiny." God had obviously withdrawn His hand from shaping the affairs of the black race in Africa.

About two months following this letter of despair, Crummell's health had so deteriorated that he had to go to Sierra Leone once more, but while there, he was told he would have to return to America if he were ever to recover his health. On April 1, 1872, he bought a passage to Boston, and on December 23, 1872, now settled in New York, he resigned from the Foreign Committee, and took on new duties of officiating over a congregation in New York City.

Crummell had worked diligently in Liberia as

missionary, high school teacher, college professor, and moral leader. He arrived in the country bubbling with enthusiasm and optimism, but he left a defeated man, physically sick and spiritually debilitated. His son, according to Blyden, was attacked and beaten by the same mob that had attacked Blyden, and the Roberts–led mulatto faction seemed firmly entrenched. With this caste problem unresolved, the Pan–African hopes of Crummell were at their lowest ebb. The optimistic and determined missionary had explored fully the notion of an international Pan–Africanism, but the idea proved to be premature. Much work still needed to be done on chauvinistic national attitudes and the blight of complexion consciousness. His spiritual vision of man, however, remained intact.

4

The Final Years

Crummell landed in America a sick man and
unsure about his future. He had not totally given up
on Liberia, and he was not well settled in New York.
He complained to his English friend, the Reverend
John Ketton, about the racial prejudices still existing
in America, and Ketton urged him to go slow on the
matter of social equality, since it took time for the
black race to "prove" itself worthy![1] Ketton was
anxious for Crummell to return to Liberia. In another
letter, after remarking on his surprise that Africa's
climate did not agree with Crummell's health, Ketton
expressed hope that Crummell would have been the
first black bishop in Liberia.[2] Crummell did express
to the Reverend John Vaughan Lewis his intention to
return to Liberia,[3] and as late as 1880, Blyden
reported that on his visit to America he had met
Crummell who had not given up the idea of returning
to Liberia.

Actually, in the early 1870s, the emigration
movement had gathered momentum once more. In
1858, Garnet had established the African Civilization
Society[4] which assisted Crummell in his
colonizationist schemes, but, in the euphoria of the
Civil War days, he had joined forces with Frederick
Douglass and Martin Delany in urging black
Americans to close ranks with the Union Army to

help save the Union. However, when in the 1870s Garnet, among others, realized that black people were being abandoned by the North to the ruthless- ness of embittered, unreconstructured Southern whites, through the African Civilization Society, he again turned to helping black people to organize themselves to emigrate to Africa. Blyden visited America in 1874 on a mission similar to the one he had undertaken twelve years earlier with Crummell, and by 1877, there were more black Americans wanting to emigrate to Liberia than at any other time since the founding of the black republic.[5] Garnet had become very active in this effort and was working under the guidance of and in collaboration with Crummell.

Crummell took the opportunity to fuel this emi- gration excitement in his address before the African International Association in 1877. He blamed Liberia's woes on those missionaries who, in their zeal to save souls, had neglected the temporal needs of the native Africans, and on the mulatto settlers who were unable or unwilling to learn from and form an "enlightened" partnership with the indigenous Africans. In effect, it would seem that Crummell was trying to encourage a band of emigrants to settle in Liberia and render powerless those missionaries and mulattoes who had sabotaged his Pan-African efforts in West Africa. Personally, he returned to Liberia only once, in 1882, to receive an honorary degree while Blyden was president of Liberia College, and he even tried to dissuade Garnet from going to Liberia.

Clearly, in spite of whatever advice he offered on emigrating to Liberia, Crummell's heart was settled in America. While he was regaining his health, he became involved with St. Mary's Church in Washing- ton, D.C. On returning to America, though he had resigned from the Foreign Mission, he still had a position with the domestic arm of this Missionary

Society which afforded him an annual appropriation of $500. In addition, he first took up duties as pastor at St. Phillip's Church in New York City, the church in which his former mentor, the Reverend Peter Williams, Jr., was once rector. However, Crummell might have heard talk about building a new church in Washington, D.C. for the all-black St. Mary's congregation.[6] When, therefore, within a few months after his return to America he was invited to take over the rectorship of St. Mary's Protestant Episcopal Church in Washington, D.C., he accepted. In fact, St. Mary's was not a church but a chapel[7] attached to St. John's Church, and the black people who attended this chapel requested a colored clergyman to be their curate. Since Crummell was contemplating his returning to Africa, he could not guarantee more than six months' service. Moreover, Bishop William Whittingham was under the misapprehension that Crummell was not in the American orders, and the suggestion that he was not a priest in the American Episcopal church greatly annoyed Crummell. Crummell testily informed the Reverend John Vaughan Lewis that he was as much a "clergyman of this church as he [Lewis] was."[8] Crummell began meeting with his St. Mary's parishioners in an informal manner, and his presence led to an increase in the membership of St. Mary's chapel.[9] By the beginning of 1873, it was official that Crummell's ill health would prevent his return to Africa,[10] and on Sunday, June 15, 1873, Crummell formally took charge of St. Mary's Chapel.[11] Among the original thirty worshipers at this chapel were Dr. Alain Locke's father and Miss Charlotte Ray, the first colored woman lawyer in the United States.

Residing in Washington, D.C., Crummell asserted himself in the nation's capital. He founded a large Sunday school, extended divine services in the vicinity of Howard University, and about twelve blocks from the university established another Sunday school room. He sought a "lay reader's license" for his assistant, and was ecstatic over the "zeal, devotedness, liberality, and harmony . . . [of] the people of St. Mary's Church."[12] Crummell established a relationship with the Commission for Colored People, which was a lay group established to oversee black Episcopalians in the Washington metropolitan area, and he soon became minister at large for all black Episcopalians in the District of Columbia. Significantly, he did not restrict his jurisdiction to the black elite residing in the downtown Washington area. As he had done in Liberia, he concerned himself with the most neglected black people. He instituted Sunday schools and divine services in the Southeast area—The Island—among the poorest of the poor.[13] In addition to his impressive work, Crummell delivered such brilliant sermons that Bishop Whittingham privately inquired of the Reverend Calbraith Perry whether he (Crummell) had the degree of Doctor of Divinity? "Yes, got it from Lincoln University."[14] Among the white clergy, among the black middle class and, most importantly, among the black masses, Crummell was making his presence felt.

Crummell was a regenerated man since his final depressing years in Liberia; however, family problems still dogged him. His wife and Sidney had remained in Liberia, and he received a letter advising him to send for his son who was squandering away his money.[15] Beyond problems with Sidney, Crummell's relationship with his wife had reached a breaking point. One can discern a basic incompatibility between Crummell and his wife very early in their marriage. The basic conflict seems to be that Mrs. Crummell was interested in personal uplift for her immediate family, and encouraged her husband to leave America "because she saw no hope for us as a family . . . in the future."[16] On the other hand, Crummell was committed to a general uplift of his American brethren. For example, when he was only seven months in England, he vowed, "I want, I desire from my inmost heart, to help upbuild my people in the U.S . . . rather than leave and go to the West Indies or Africa, where I had liberal offers made to me."[17] He felt that his wife, whom he proudly described as "a woman of first-rate capacity" who "took off all the prizes, in Reading, Arithmetic and Grammar" in the common school for black girls in New York and afterward became a teacher,[18] would change her mind once she received further educational training in England. He was convinced that she would share *his* dream of returning to America to help educate their less fortunate brothers and sisters. It is obvious that Mrs. Crummell never abandoned her more personal concerns in favor of the Pan-African ideals of her husband. When his wife joined him in the United States, she submitted charges against him to Bishop Whittingham.[19] The nature of the charges was not spelled out, but they probably centered around neglect, as Sidney's letter in Liberia had suggested. Bishop Whittingham passed on the charges to his assistant, Bishop William Pinkney, and on November 14, 1874, Bishop Pinkney wrote Bishop Whittingham, "I am satisfied he [Crummell] is all right."[20] Bishop Pinkney was very sympathetic toward Crummell ("He had a hard trial to endure, poor fellow"), but he decided to get all the facts from references Crummell had given him of people in Liberia and the United States. After all of the facts were examined, Crummell was allowed to get a divorce and continue as an Episcopal priest. A sad chapter in Crummell's life had come to an end.

Six years later, Crummell got married for a second time. On September 23, 1880, the Reverend Alexander Crummell was married to Jennie M. Simpson at St. Phillip's Church in New York City. The Reverend Atwell, then rector at Crummell's old church, performed the ceremony, and one of the witnesses was an old African Free School graduate,

Charles L. Reason. At St. Luke's, Jennie actively supported the efforts of her husband. Miss Helen Moore, who had known the Crummell family personally, in an interview described Jennie as "the power behind the throne." Jennie would aid and help supervise many of the church activities, and in her will she "provided for aged widows and spinsters of African descent."[21] In 1886, while Crummell was ailing, he wrote of Jennie, "I want *her* company amidst my delights." Throughout the rest of Crummell's life, Jennie Morris Simpson remained his devoted and loyal wife.

Pretty well settled in a job and in his domestic situation, Crummell was able once more to give his attention to his Pan–African mission. In America, as in his later years in Liberia, his Pan–African focus was on self–development and black solidarity. No longer was he promoting the union of black Americans with native Africans through any emigration or colonization scheme. He was fully reconciled to the fact that black Americans were part of the American landscape and were there to stay: "When a RACE . . . numbering, perchance, some eight or ten millions—once enters a land and settles therein as its home and heritage, then occurs an event as fixed and abiding as the rooting of the Pyrenees in Spain or the Alps in Italy."[22] The black man was intricately woven into the fabric of the American society, and to attempt to extricate him was tantamount to destroying the entire society. "By [the] black man [the nation] stands or falls,"[23] Crummell prophesized. This was a different Crummell from the one who in the 1850s and 1860s had championed the colonization of Africa by American Blacks. Now his eyes were turned to the American national scene, and he embarked upon a program of self–determination and unity among black people.

Four major areas may be identified in Crummell's plan of action for black self–help: (1) the establishment of black institutions; (2) the mobilization of the black masses; (3) the grooming of an appropriate black leadership; and (4) the organization of an educational program fitted to the needs of black people. This four-point agenda gained its direction and substance from Crummell's life experiences.

ESTABLISHMENT OF BLACK INSTITUTIONS

As was the case when he first arrived in Liberia, Crummell's attention during his first years in Washington, D.C. was directed to the erecting of a church building. Around this church building activity, which called for a separate church for black Episcopalians in Washington, D.C., Crummell's Pan-African ideas of the founding of black institutions were expressed.

Hope for a racially unified nation had glimmered among black leaders in the immediate post-Civil War period. With the passage of the Thirteenth (1865), Fourteenth (1863), and Fifteenth (1870) Amendments, all black Americans were legally free, acknowledged to be American citizens with equal protection under the law, and no longer denied the right to vote. Black people were elected to the U.S. Congress (between 1869–1877, fourteen different black men were at various times members of the House of Representatives and two were senators), black universities were established, and, generally speaking, there was a euphoric feeling of hope among black people during this era of Reconstruction. Gradually, however, the 1866 fervor of the Radical Reconstructionists was cooling, and by 1871, the early supporters of the Reconstruction were proclaiming, "The experiment has totally failed."[24]

When Crummell returned to America in 1872, he found a situation in which the black man was at best neglected; at worst, harassed. The black man was in a state of "in-betweenity"—free from slavery, but not enjoying full freedom and equality. Crummell saw his job as similar to what it was in Liberia—to help establish a program of self-development. Pan-Africanism meant black self-development. He realized that in regard to black people, the country was in "an ebb tide of indifference"; the nation was focusing on reestablishing a union of North and South. In a famous address, "The Social Principle," he warned black Americans in 1875: "the anxiety for union neutralized the interest in the black man."[25] Thus, when in the spring of 1877 President Hayes withdrew the federal troops from the South and restored home rule, this "betrayal of the Negro" was no sudden whim of a president.[26] Crummell had correctly placed his hand on the pulse of the nation's attitude toward black people two years before the tragic withdrawal.

Fully aware that black people as a group had to look after their own welfare, the Freedman's Bureau having ceased all operations by 1872, Crummell advocated that black people not sacrifice their black institutions on the altar of integration. To surrender their black schools, black churches, black associations and black societies, all in the name of integration was a dangerous heresy. With the absorption of the African Free schools, where Crummell, Garnet, James McCune Smith and others had gotten their first training, into the New York public school system, no distinctive black leaders were coming forward as they did in the early decades of the nineteenth century. In almost scornful language, Crummell condemned as folly the breaking up of black organizations "under the flighty stimulants of imaginative conceit."[27]

Crummell's undertaking of the building of a black church signaled his belief in the need for black institutions. Undaunted by the bad experience he had with the building of Trinity Church in Liberia, he proceeded to replace St. Mary's Chapel with the first black Protestant Episcopal church in Washington, D.C. The Protestant Episcopal church diocese of Maryland not only agreed with Crummell's idea but encouraged Episcopalians everywhere to aid with the funds.[28] On June 13, 1876, Crummell had printed an appeal to churchmen to help erect "a Church for a most needy people." The church must not be "small and pitiful," but a "big, strong arm to the Diocese." The District of Columbia was not only the nation's capital, it had over 43,000 black citizens, and was the home of the distinguished black institution, Howard University. Moreover, the city had hundreds of professional black people. There was undoubtedly a need for a black, independent church, but the churches in Washington, D.C. could not carry the whole burden. The appeal was formally approved by both Bishop Whittingham and his assistant Bishop Pinkney.[29] Crummell's dream of an independent, black church had become a "National Church Enterprise." In July 1876, ground was broken and the foundation laid for a new church. By November 9, 1876, Bishop Pinkney duly laid the cornerstone.[30]

Though this black church was to be the result of principally black effort, Crummell did not shun white support. He actively sought assistance from the white Episcopal church body. In describing the state of black America, he had used the phrase "a nation within a nation,"[31] but he had not meant by that the building of a separate black Episcopal church. He endorsed the concept that black Episcopal churches ought to organize themselves into "a society for systematic church extension among Colored People," by increasing the number of black candidates for Holy Orders, and by multiplying the number of churches to meet the needs of black Episcopalians "but free of caste."[32] Accordingly, when Crummell set about to demonstrate his Pan-African tenet of black self-development, he was seeking merely to add a black Episcopal "arm" to the Maryland diocese.

Due to a shortage of funds, building plans for the new church did not proceed as fast as Crummell had hoped. On January 11, 1877, he wrote a desperate note to Bishop Whittingham: "Just now we are at a standstill, our money being all spent."[33] Crummell might have feared the Trinity Church problems of Liberia repeating themselves in America. To prevent any prolonged delay in the building plans, he set out on a fund-raising lecture tour in the northern and eastern states. It was a successful venture. In the 1877 annual report of the Maryland diocese at the Convocation of Washington, the Reverend Meyer Levin was happy to report that Dr. Crummell, after three months' work of fund raising, returned "with over ninety pledges [of fifty dollars each] . . . and with promise of future aid, so as to make it almost certain that he will be able to finish St. Luke's Church."[34] Indeed, work resumed on the church building.

On Thanksgiving Day, November 25, 1879, the first divine services were held at St. Luke's Episcopal Church, Washington, D.C., and the Reverend Alexander Crummell preached. For his text Crummell used: "This is none other than the house of God and this is the gate of heaven." In his sermon, he made two significant observations which underscored the actions of this holy man throughout his life. First, he pointed out that "the house of God" must not only be lavish in its material splendor, be it a temple of a former age or a greegree house of West Africa, but it must also exude a spiritual element—God's presence. It was this spiritual element that Crummell described as "the distinctive constituent" of a church. This spiritual presence was always real to Crummell. The other observation in this Thanksgiving Day sermon worth noting was Crummell's deep concern for the poor and often overlooked masses. Contrasting St. Luke's with the princely churches of the English Tudor period, he observed: "It [St. Luke's] is not the gift of a king, but it is the gift of large and princely souls."[35] At this point in the sermon, he gave a list of the various walks of life that contributed to this church building effort, but singled out for special recongnition the laboring classes, the poor people from his parish. Crummell had grounded his Pan-African vision on the unification of better-off blacks with the less fortunate, less advanced members of the black race. Standing and preaching in St. Luke's Episcopal Church, he, at last, had fulfilled the dream he had had in the 1840s when he had gone to England to raise funds. It must be noted, however, that there was no formal consecration because there was still indebtedness on the church.

Yet Crummell was able to stand proud, confident that the social principle, as exemplified in racial cooperation, was responsible for this splendid achievement. Not only was this effort indicative of church solidarity (there has been an impressive history of black church solidarity in America), but it demonstrated the effectiveness of collective social action as well. The church was designed by a black man (Crummell himself), the plans were drawn by a black man (Calvin T.S. Brent, the first black architect of the District of Columbia), the funds were almost entirely raised by black men and women soliciting donations from their fellow black citizens (Mr. John W. Cromwell had organized The Sinking Fund of St. Mary's to raise funds), the rector and parishioners were black, and in 1879, the name was changed from St. Mary's to St. Luke's as chosen by black Episcopalians.[36] This was not a separate black church, but a black congregation, through self-effort, asserting its independence *within* the Episcopal church institution.

But there was trouble at St. Luke's. A mulatto-led faction in the church was trying to replace Crummell as rector. It was a replay of the

Liberian experience, with one significant exception—
this time Crummell was supported by his bishop. The
problem was a power–struggle between Crummell and
the vestry. The vestry were laymen duly elected by
the church members to assist the pastor in carrying
out the duties of the church. However, on March 28,
1882, St. Luke's vestry sent a letter to Bishop
Pinkney requesting the dissolution of the Reverend
Crummell's rectorship.[37] They listed several reasons
for their decision and twice referred to the rector's
"cold and repulsive manner" which the congregation
was merely tolerating. The true cause of their
complaint, however, dated back to 1879, when
Crummell refused to accede to their request and
appoint Mr. C.A. Fleetwood as choirmaster. In a
twenty–six page letter to Bishop Pinkney, Crummell
stated decisively: "On this issue [the appointment of
Fleetwood], . . . I am prepared, in my old age, after
nigh forty years service in the Church, to go out of
St. Luke's, to poverty, to silence, it may be to
disgrace: but my conscience will not suffer me to
appoint any such man as Fleetwood as my choir
leader and master."[38] Mr. Fleetwood was formerly
the choir master at St. Mary's Chapel. He often got
into conflict with Crummell about the appropriate
hymns to sing at various services. A few days before
the opening of the new St. Luke's Church, Fleetwood
resigned from the choir without giving any notice.
Crummell resented the fact that Fleetwood, a former
Presbyterian church member, presumed to suggest to
him how to conduct his services.

    In addition to Fleetwood, Crummell identified
three other members of the vestry as the real
troublemakers. As Crummell reported it, one was "a
disturber of the peace" who was "kicked out of the
Presbyterian Church"; another was a notorious
libertine who was forced, "at the point of a pistol," to
marry a young girl whom he had debauched; the third
troublemaker was a well–known drunkard who lived in

open adultery with a harlot. As he had drawn on Edward Blyden in Liberia to attest to his claims against the characters of others, so in America he cited Frederick Douglass as a witness to the characters of the men whom he condemned.

Bishop Pinkney placed the matter in the hands of the Committee on Colored Workers and requested of them a written recommendation. On May 2, 1882, a majority[39] of the committee voted for Crummell's resignation. The resolution read in part: "Because of long continued troubles that cannot seem to be resolved . . . [be it resolved that] the Ecclesiastical relations between Dr. Crummell and St. Luke's Church be severed . . . in such manner as will not injure his reputation or impair the integrity of his clerical character."[40]

Had the resolution calling for the Reverend Crummell's resignation stood, it would certainly have served a deadly blow to his morale. Fortunately, however, on the day following the resolution of the committee, Bishop Pinkney announced that the Standing Committee of the diocese, after examination of the evidence, unanimously decided not to dissolve the Reverend Crummell's relation with St. Luke's. It was the second time within two years,[41] that Bishop Pinkney had come out in support of Crummell against the vestry. This kind of support from his bishop gave Crummell new hope, but the vestry did not relent in its harassment of Crummell. On February 6, 1883, the vestry sent a letter to Bishop Pinkney complaining that Crummell was "making material alterations of the basement at St. Luke's" without consulting them.[42] Nothing came of their complaint. Crummell had won out in this power struggle.

However, Crummell's problems extended beyond the vestry. The annual appropriation of $500 which he was receiving from the Mission Committee was to be discontinued in 1878 because Bishop Whittingham had

not requested that it be retained.[43] Bishop
Whittingham was probably reluctant to request con-
tinuance of the appropriation because of a minor
conflict he was having with Crummell at that time.
Yielding to the anti-Crummell faction at St. Mary's
Chapel, the bishop refused to allow Crummell to
retain an assistant. Crummell knew that Bishop
Whittingham was being influenced by the vestry, so
he had a petition, requesting that "Rev. A.A. Roberts
be retained as assistant to Dr. Crummell," sent to the
bishop. The petition was signed by several active
church members in his congregation, including his
son, Sidney, and his brother, Charles.[44] The bishop,
however, was guided by the recommendation of the
Committee on Colored Workers in D.C.: "It is not
expedient at this time to employ Reverend Mr.
Roberts."[45] Crummell remained a thorn in the
bishop's side. The following year he wrote to Bishop
Whittingham requesting monetary aid for one of his
candidates to the priesthood.[46] Again, the bishop did
not heed Crummell's request, for five months later
the candidate was writing to Bishop Whittingham,
repeating his request for aid.[47]

   In 1880, Crummell posed a more difficult problem
for the bishop. Crummell sought to have young black
girls from his parish set up an official, associate
branch of the Girls [sic] Friendly Society. This
Friendly Society functioned under the direction of
the Protestant Episcopal church and claimed as its
goal, "helping the young and weak and ignorant."[48]
The problem was that the Girls Friendly Society was
an all-white organization. Moreover, other denominations, like the Roman Catholic church, were
admitting black girls into their sodalities. The
Episcopal church could be placed in an embarrassing
position. Crummell was aware of the church's
vulnerable position, but he gave no publicity to the
application of "his girls."[49] Significantly, five months
after Crummell's application to the Girls Friendly

Society, Bishop Pinkney supported Crummell for the first time against the vestry. There is no indication in the correspondence of either Crummell or Pinkney of the outcome of the application to join the Girls Friendly Society.

Secure in his authority at St. Luke's, Crummell sought to expand his ideas on self-development within the church. In 1883, he set about organizing a Conference of Church Workers Among Colored People. Through this religious organization, he was setting up a model for black political leaders to emulate. Douglass, in 1883, at the Louisville convention had described himself as "an uneasy Republican." Crummell's solution to this dilemma of uneasiness was self-reliance. He proposed that black churches of a particular denomination in a particular diocese should organize and govern themselves subject only to the ruling parent body of that denomination. The existing structure, in which black congregations were always subordinated to their fellow white congregations who represented the diocese at national conventions, displayed a master-slave arrangement which was particularly distasteful to Crummell. He had removed St. Mary's Chapel from the status of a satellite to the white St. John's Church and had established the independent black St. Luke's Church on an equal footing with St. John's. Now he sought to unify all the black churches and pull them out of the patronizing control of white churches. He insisted that black churches should represent themselves at all general conferences.[50] Crummell was not seeking separation of the races as much as he was promoting elevation of the black race so that it could integrate on its own terms on the higher levels of society. This consolidation of the black race, this withdrawal into a unit, was the strategy proposed by Crummell in economics, politics, and education. Black power, for Crummell, meant black unity. And black unity meant Pan-

Africanism, and Pan-Africanism ultimately meant human unity. This version of the basic social principle was always clear to Crummell. It was in this spirit of ultimate human brotherhood that Crummell accepted the post of president of the Colored Ministers' Union of Washington and agreed to be a member of the Commission for Church Work Among Colored People.[51]

His tenure at St. Luke's was fraught with difficulties and hardship. "It has been a hard and terrible field," he wrote to his friend, the Reverend Frazier Miller in Charleston, Virginia.[52] He was very disappointed when Miller was not chosen as his successor at St. Luke's: "Washington needs *you*!"[53] But the forces in control at St. Luke's wanted a weak man: "The old set here wanted 'putty' not a man!"[54] He urged Miller not to "let up" and to have faith in the ordinary members of the congregation: *"Some good people you must have. Organize them."*[55] In letter after letter, Crummell encouraged his friend to "stick" to his calling. When Miller was removed from his position at Charleston, Crummell uplifted his spirit: "If a man keeps hammering, with the Gospel, in the poorest place, he will change and build up that place, to the glory of God, and the salvation of men."[56] In another letter, he pointed out that the new black leader in the church has to be prepared to endure many ordeals. Referring to his own stewardship, which came to an end at St. Luke's in 1894, Crummell wrote: "I have been fighting with the beasts of Ephesus twenty-two years . . . *not* the people, but a clique of half-educated gentlemen, . . . but I did not run away."[57]

The building of St. Luke's was more than merely erecting a physical structure for black Episcopalians. The establishment of a black congregation confirmed and reinforced Crummell's faith in the rank and file, and this confidence in the masses played a prominent role in his Pan-African plans.

MOBILIZATION OF THE BLACK MASSES

The inclusion and mobilization of the black masses in a self-help program proved to be a complicated problem. First, the black educated middle-class had to be convinced that the only road to effective self-development lay in group solidarity. Second, and going hand-in-hand with this need for black unity, black leaders needed to be persuaded that the conservation of the black race required safeguarding. Underlying both these concerns were the concept of integration and "the mulatto complex."

Crummell had learned his lesson in Liberia. He had gone to Africa with the notion that the Talented Tenth who were trained in America would pull up to their civilized level the native Africans. However, he had found his greatest support among the unlettered Africans, and, by the time he was leaving Africa, he felt sure that, if Liberia were to realize its potential greatness, the native Africans had to provide the guiding hand. In America, he translated his trust in the native Africans into one of his abiding principles: "Only when the masses . . . were marshalled" could any effort triumph.[58] Crummell had grown into the understanding that great *thought* might issue from *individual* achievement, but great *action* resulted from *collective* effort.

Thus, there was room for both the individual and the masses in Crummell's scheme of thought. The role of individuals, of the Talented Tenth, was to generate thought and expose ideas; however, only the masses acting with common concerns could implement any program and provide lasting direction for the group. Were American society one people, not divided along the lines of race, Crummell would have been the first to urge collective action on the part of black and white Americans alike. However, he knew too well that prejudice had poisoned the mind of white America beyond any hope for immediate union of white and black societies: "Nine-tenths of the American people have become so poisoned and stimulated by the noxious influence of caste, that . . . they would resist to the utmost before they would allow the affiliations . . . that implied the social or domestic principles."[59] The grim fact of the matter in the mid-1870s was that black people were separated, isolated from the mainstream of white America.

The spirit of Reconstruction had moved many black leaders to pursue integration as the final solution of the black problem. At a National Convention for Colored People (popularly known as the Reconstruction Convention) called in Washington, D.C. in 1873, two items had dominated the agenda—the enforcement of the Fifteenth Amendment which guaranteed the right to vote to all black people, and national support for Charles Sumner's civil rights bill.[60] The real thrust of the integration movement favored individual "integration by merit." George Washington Cable had recommended this kind of individual integration based on class. Cable, who grew up in New Orleans fully aware of Haitian-descended *gens de couleur* of wealth and refinement, promoted class rather than race separation, and so he argued that a well-bred, well-educated man should, indeed, share social rank with a white man of similar breeding and education.[61]

In response to this growing mood for horizontal integration across racial lines, Crummell preached vertical union of middle-class Blacks with the masses of black people. He implored the better-off Blacks to assist the deprived and degraded members of the race. "The poor forsaken ones in the lanes and alleys and cellars of the great cities," he pleaded, "stand by them."[62] With penetrating sociological insight, Crummell was one of the first to point out that the freedman did not, with the stroke of the pen, become free of all the accumulated and ingrained deficiencies that slavery had bred into him. As he put it, "The evil of gross and monstrous abominations, the evil of great organic institutions crop out long after the departure of the institutions themselves."[63] Yet, the black victims of the abominable institution of slavery had an essential role to play in the regeneration of the black race. Consequently, Crummell appealed to a graduating class of black college students at Storer College to "go down to the humblest conditions of [the] race, and carry to their lowly huts and cabins all the resources of science . . . political economics . . . [and] the appliances of school."[64] The primary task facing the few fortunate Blacks who were educated and enjoyed a measure of success consisted in spreading their knowledge among the untutored masses and joining with them in a grand self-help effort. Crummell demanded even more from the "colored women" who through "a merciful providence" had acquired a measure of "refinement and civilization." He urged them to form a band of sisters of mercy to make prolonged visits to the plantation homes of their black sisters and be prepared to lie down and die, "exhausted by their labors."[65] On a personal level, Crummell bound himself "as 'with hooks of steel' to the most degraded class in the land, my own 'kinsmen according to the flesh.'"[66]

"Kinsmen according to the flesh" remained a lasting Pan-African principle with Crummell to his dying day. Race was no geographical accident, but, like all other human conditions, it was the working out of "God's hand in history."[67] But Crummell's attitude toward race must not be construed as racism in the modern sense of the word, though driven to an extreme position in defense of the black man's humanity, Crummell did speak of "the destined superiority of the Negro."[68] To Crummell, the principle of unity which held the universe together had a balancing "conserving power which tended everywhere to fixity of type,"[69] and so races were meant to retain their "type." American society would mature only when it could accommodate a hetero- geneity of races, only when it had become, what a modern sociologist would term, "a pluralistic society." In this sense and this sense alone can Crum- mell be classified a believer in race. As an old man in the 1890s, he explained to young black university students at the Garnet Lyceum of Lincoln University that "there is nothing more abiding, nothing more persistent than race, and race peculiarities."[70] If a feeling of racial solidarity could be fostered in the breasts of middle-class Blacks, then, "not . . . mindless of the brotherhood of the entire species . . . but urged by the feeling of kinship,"[71] they would stand behind and support the degraded masses of people.

Kinship, for Crummell, included anyone who had African blood coursing through his veins, and this broad definition of race led to charges by Edward Blyden that Crummell feared the mulattoes.[72] But this charge was not true. As we have already noted, he did acknowledge that Liberia's problems stemmed from the mulattoes, but, instead of becoming "a fanatical opponent of mulattoes," as Blyden did,[73] Crummell sought to heal the misguided and debili- tating split between the two groups. Reconciled to the fact that black Americans were in America to stay, Crummell realized that the black race could ill afford a split along any lines. But Blyden remained steadfast in his distrust of mulattoes, and on an 1889 visit to America urged pure black Americans to return to Africa. He openly attacked mulattoes and was in turn condemned for creating divisiveness among the black people in America. Crummell undoubtedly was among these who had censured Blyden's activities.

Notwithstanding his conciliatory approach toward the "coloreds," Crummell's racial doctrines inevitably led to a head–on collision with mulatto–thinking Blacks. To those who sought the assimilation of the black race into white society, he was uncompromising and insisted that "The race–problem cannot be settled by extinction of the race."[74] He openly blasted those leaders who felt that the abandonment of race concepts was essential to achieve integration: "That the colored people of this country should forget . . . that they ARE colored people. . . . Turn madman and go into a lunatic asylum, and then, per chance, you may forget it! . . . The only place I know of in this land where you can 'forget that you are colored' is the grave!"[75] Always thinking of the black man in terms of race first and nationality second, Crummell berated those blacks who avoided the use of the word "African" and espoused the term "Afro–American." In a letter to his young journalist friend John E. Bruce, he rhetorically asked, "What is the reason our journalists are so afraid of race–designation in their newspapers and journals?" And later in the letter, he condemned "that bastard, milk and water term—the Afro–American."[76] As he grew older, Crummell grew more contemptuous of those colored people who had remained in "complexion cliques," and in a letter to Bruce dated November 11, 1895, he bitterly observed: "Those colored Negro–haters are beneath contempt."[77] Crummell died believing that the only way a black man could be a dignified American citizen was by deliberately and consciously claiming his Africanness and joining with the black masses in an effort to uplift the entire race.

The fight for racial solidarity placed Crummell in awkward positions with regard to civil and political matters. In his 1875 address, "The Social Principle," he had clearly come out against those who advocated agitation and protest for civil rights. For laws that needed to be enacted or changed, agitation was a sensible strategy, but the fight for the right to sleep in public hotels and to visit exhibitions in public theaters, Crummell placed very low on the agenda for black self-uplift. Crummell's self-pride would not allow him to force himself to intermingle with white people who disdained his company, and he acidly observed: "There is something ignoble in any man, any class, any race of men whining and crying because they cannot move in spheres where they are not wanted."[78] Somewhat naïvely, Crummell reasoned that racists must eliminate racism! Since he was not a racist, he argued that it was not his responsibility to destroy the "caste system" in America. "My work is special to my own people," he explained, and separated himself from "that class of colored men" who thought it their business to try to get white America to change its racist ways.[79] In political affairs, too, Crummell placed little trust. To the graduating class of Storer College, with an unmistakable tinge of sarcasm in his tone of voice, he challenged the students and undoubtedly Frederick Douglass who was in the audience to "leave for *a little while* at least, all idea of being President of the United States."[80] He maintained this distrust in politics as the solution to the black problem throughout his life, for as late as 1896, he was impatiently writing to Bruce "so the election will come and go and *then*, we can all turn our undivided attention to race matters."[81]

The appeal to race matters at the expense of civil and political rights did not mean a passive acceptance of the black status quo. It is quite true that Crummell never took as aggressive an approach of protest and agitation in social problems as Douglass did, but he certainly did not support Booker T. Washington's laissez-faire solution that "The best course to pursue in regard to the civil rights bill in the South is to let it alone."[82] In labor affairs, Crummell incited black people to "strive; push; argue; protest; remonstrate; demand" to be admitted to workshops of mechanics.[83] Nor did he go to the extreme that Blyden did in condemning black Americans' participation in the political process. In a letter to the Reverend Francis J. Grimké, Blyden had written: "It seems to me that if I lived in this country I should scrupulously avoid politics and everything leading to politics."[84] Crummell, on the other hand, as he gradually recognized the absolute importance for every black American to enjoy all the civil and political rights accorded to American citizens, advocated, in the spirit of Douglass, that "this country should be agitated and even convulsed till . . . every man in the land is guaranteed fully every civil and political right and prerogative."[85]

When Crummell played down civil and political rights, it was to redirect attention to the black masses. He quite accurately saw that the immediate gain of access to public hotels and theaters would benefit chiefly the fortunate few Afro–Americans who had achieved a measure of status within America. These fortunate few were mainly colored Americans who made up about one–eighth of the black population. The masses of black people had known nothing but "unlettered rudeness" for over two hundred years. The kind of integration that Crummell favored was the colored man's integration into the despicable conditions of his downtrodden black brothers.

It was also in the spirit of black solidarity that Crummell promoted his ideas on race. We must remember that when Crummell spoke about the destined superiority of the black race, he was contending with white racists like the Reverend Dr. J. L. Tucker.* But also in a private letter, Crummell had

---

*Tucker had presented a paper arguing the innate moral inferiority of the black race, and Crummell had demolished his arguments in his celebrated "Defense of the Negro Race."

confirmed his faith in the black masses: "There is no race of people on the American soil who have greater native genius than this race of ours."[86] On another occasion, he identified this native genius as the black man's ability to glide "into the traits of his neighbors."[87] Given this eclectic quality, Crummell confidently predicted that "Nothing . . . on earth . . . can keep back this destined advance of the Negro race."[88] The vigorous promotion of such a race concept was vital to any black solidarity program.

Crummell's views on self–development and black solidarity were gaining respect in some black circles. He gathered around him a group of young men who looked up to him for leadership. This group included John Welsey Cromwell, a teacher in the Washington public schools and a newspaper publisher; John E. Bruce, a black nationalist journalist who wrote under the pseudonym "Bruce Grit"; and Paul Laurence Dunbar, the black poet and novelist. In the same year that Crummell delivered his address on the social principle, black newspaper editors held a national convention in Cincinnati. It became clear at this convention that Crummell was emerging as one of the leaders of black American thought. Self–reliance, united action, education, and the acquisition of land were outlined as the program of action that would save the black race in America. Agitation and political activity were downplayed, and group self–help was emphasized.[89] Clearly, the stage was being set for the emergence of Booker T. Washington, and Crummell was laying the cornerstone for Washington's stage even as he was literally laying the cornerstone for his St. Luke's Episcopal Church in 1876. At another National Convention of Colored People held in Nashville, Tennessee, in 1879, one of the delegates declared in open language that "race unity [among black people] is the all–important factor." One of Crummell's close friends, John W. Cromwell, advanced wealth as the source of greatness for the black race. Black newspapers across the nation pointed in the direction of Crummell's social principle. Operating out of Crummell's home city, Washington, D.C., the militant Washington *Bee*, a black newspaper, appealed to its black readers to patronize black business.

In the midst of this ground swell of support, Crummell's program suffered a setback. Within two months after his appeal to the colored female leadership to focus attention on lending a helping hand to Southern Blacks rather than fighting for civil rights, the Supreme Court, on October 15, 1883, ruled that the Civil Rights Act of 1875 was unconstitutional. The Court's decision was a blow to the hopes of the very colored leadership that Crummell was addressing. T. Thomas Fortune, perhaps the leading black journalist of the day, in reaction to this Supreme Court ruling, began an editorial in the New York *Globe* thus: "The colored people of the United States feel today as if they had been baptized in ice water."[90] The colored leadership could not help but feel Crummell's views had played some part in influencing the Court's decision. It was no surprise, therefore, to find Fortune, in his book *Black and White*, published the year following the rescinding of the black people's civil rights, directly attacking the theocratic determinism which had been the foundation for all of Crummell's thoughts: "The talk about the black people being brought to this country to prepare themselves to evangelize Africa is so much religious nonsense boiled down to sycophantic platitude . . . black people of this country are Americans, not Africans."[91]

On the matter of education, Fortune rejected outright the separate school system though he did concur with Crummell that elementary and industrial education was what the colored people in the South stood most in need of.[92] In the area of politics, Fortune was clear in his position: "Let there be no aim of *solidifying* the colored vote."[93] In fact, he urged black people to feel no longer bound to the Republican party. In general, Fortune very idealistically encouraged the union of black and white labor. Crummell saw such unification as an end, but he felt the more immediate need was unification within the black race. Fortune was pointing a new direction which leaned towards Marxism.

Crummell certainly would not accept the materialistic basis of Marxism, but there was much in this philosophy that was similar to Crummellian thought. In his Jubilate address, he spoke of "a Divine, an infinite, and all-powerful hand which moves in all our history; and it moves for good! Incidentally, it allows severity and anguish; but its primary trend is redemptive and saving."[94] Marx's belief in a fundamental cosmic law underlying all of history could have appealed to Crummell; also, the emphasis in Marxist thought on the importance of the masses of exploited workers was directly in keeping with Crummell's concern for the despised and forgotten black men and women in the alleys of cities and the broken down huts on plantations. Finally, the doctrine of communism, of mankind living as one large communal family, fitted in well with Crummell's doctrine of the social principle. However, the thrust of Fortune's Marxist teachings was to achieve integration between white and black, and never once in his book did Fortune address the problem of integration between the coloreds and the blacks within the Afro-American community. Crummell several years later would dismiss Fortune as a "poet, fiddler, ruffian and buffoon."[95]

GROOMING OF A BLACK LEADERSHIP

With the arrival of young black thinkers like Fortune on the American scene, Crummell correctly realized that a new direction had to be pointed out for the black race if his Pan–African ideal was to stay alive. He had entitled his Storer College address in 1885, "The Need of New Ideas and New Aims for a New Era," but there was nothing new in what Crummell had to say. His call was for black people to shift "general thought from past servitude, to duty and service." Douglass, who was present in the audience, stood up and retaliated, "a constant recollection of the slavery of their race and [its] wrongs" must always be part of black men's history.[96] Douglass was not against Crummell's program of self effort, but he refused to allow black people to accept all blame for their condition, and he insisted that the American nation owed black Americans more than they could ever be paid. Douglass was quite right in being adamant that black people must never forget, and never allow the American people to forget, the shame of slavery which is part of American history. Only with a steady backward glance can one truly see what lies ahead.

Evidently, there was a crisis in the black leadership which needed to be addressed. Some years earlier, in the eulogy delivered for his dear childhood friend, Henry Highland Garnet, who died in Liberia in 1881, Crummell attempted to rally black America around a common leadership, be it a colored Douglass or a pure black Garnet.

Calling for greater solidarity among black leaders, Crummell used the occasion of the loss of Garnet to shore up the credibility of Frederick Douglass, then under a cloud for his association with the Republican party. Crummell saw Douglass as a man whose name "cannot die in the remembrance of the black race in this country, nor in the annals of the republic."[97] Furthermore, Crummell rebuked the younger black leaders who seemed to have thought that Douglass was "a mere bagatelle."[98] Since the latter half of the 1870s blacks had been challenging, in a serious manner, the automatic acceptance of the Republican party of which Douglass was a star supporter.[99] However, Crummell did not see that rising wave of hostility towards Douglass as an opportunity for personal advancement as the leader of black Americans. Instead, consistent with his program for racial solidarity, he countered this growing antagonism towards Douglass with his personal endorsement and admiration for the great black leader.

In the case of Garnet, Crummell reproached the black community for not accepting this great black man as their leader.[100] Garnet was a no–nonsense, aggressive black leader who as a teenager had exchanged musket shots with the "Canaan ruffians" and had organized his schoolmates to spend July 4 holidays, not celebrating, but planning a physical onslaught on the Southern plantation owners. In his famous 1843 address, he had recommended armed insurrection as the way to end slavery. Yet this brave and courageous man left for Africa feeling unappreciated among his black brothers in America. This was not a blow against mulattoes, but a direct attack against that blight for which black people were noted—"the lack of a cooperative spirit."[101]

Garnet had represented Crummell's ideal Pan–African leader. Not only had Garnet labored for his people in America, but he had also worked as a missionary in Jamaica, and finally, had died in Africa. This concern on the part of Garnet for the black world, irrespective of geographical or national boundaries, certainly appealed to the Pan–African mind of Crummell. Yet, ironically, Crummell had tried to dissuade Garnet from accepting the post of minister resident to the Republic of Liberia.[102] Fortunately, Garnet did accept the post. At Garnet's funeral, Pan–Africanism triumphed. The entire military force of Monrovia, the president and his cabinet, professors and students of Liberia College, the college president, large bodies of people from river settlements, all came and paid tribute to this great black man from America. Garnet, like W.E.B. Du Bois in Ghana much later, was accorded a state funeral.

Only after his retirement from the rectorship of St. Luke's in 1894 could Crummell devote full attention to the question of black leadership. He resented the new class of colored men, "unthinking men, who presume to lead the Negro race . . . but who in their heart of hearts, despise the Negro."[103] In a letter to John Bruce, he showed disgust for Bishop Turner's contemptible sneer at "the good for nothing Negroes,"[104] and in another letter, he expressed how upset he was about the problem of caste within the black race.[105] Crummell wanted to keep men like T. Thomas Fortune, "that Negro hater,"[106] from assuming leadership of the race. Crummell was particularly hard on Fortune, for he felt that Fortune must know "there can be nothing legitimate in associating with the whites."[107]

Bruce encouraged Crummell to come forward and assume the new leadership role. Crummell explained that the complete loss of sight in one eye[108] and the need for his church salary would not permit him to go "politically public."[109] He admitted to having strong political convictions, "and the trend is all 'Republican.'"[110] However, he placed his hope for a new black leadership in men like John Bruce and Paul Laurence Dunbar: "I look upon him [Dunbar] and yourself [Bruce] as the rising hopes of our people."[111] Crummell saw Bruce as "the gadfly" needed to keep the race thinking straight, and he assured Bruce, "God has given you great capacity for good."[112] He avidly read Bruce's editorials and applauded the young black writer's attack on the new caste system "which has no room for folks like me."[113] Crummell was gleeful when Bruce attacked Fortune and Turner. "These fellows are simply opportunists," Crummell wrote.[114]

However, Crummell knew that true leadership was not built on attacking opponents. Fortune had published his *Black and White*; now Crummell urged Bruce to publish a *Negro Reader* which would include essays by Samuel Ringgold Ward, Charles Lenox Remond, Frederick Douglass, Henry Highland Garnet, and others of that quality. Declining Bruce's invitation to write the introduction to the *Reader*, Crummell encouraged Bruce: "*You* write your own introduction . . . you don't need me."[115] He directed Bruce to William Lloyd Garrison's *Liberator* and *Emancipator* for speeches by great black orators, and referred his young protégé to John W. Cromwell: "No man in the land can aid you so much as he."[116]

In addition to this intellectual advice on getting a book published, Crummell warned Bruce to be ever on the alert against a hostile white society. He praised Bruce for keeping his eyes fixed on the fact that "the civilization under which we live is *white*."[117] Even within the church black people still were treated with scant courtesy, and Crummell assured Bruce, "The white clergy don't want a black man in any of their pulpits."[118] He insisted that young black leaders must stand proud and not demean themselves trying to get accepted by white America. For example, he was deeply annoyed at William Dean Howells's patronizing introduction to Paul Laurence Dunbar's first book of poems, *Lyrics of Lowly Life*: "Howells's critique on Dunbar filled me with indignation; but my indignation was hotter against the 'coloured sycophants,' who went crazy over his beastly patronage of the poet."[119]

More important than either intellectual effort or race consciousness, the black leader must have faith in the black masses. Crummell's new leader must not display contempt for the masses as Bishop Turner did, nor must he feel that the black masses' only hope lay in integration with the white masses, as Fortune suggested. Only months before he died, Crummell pointed out to Bruce that every black leader must recognize that his leadership worth had come directly from the masses. He wrote: "I am not writing so much for 'Bruce Grit,' as for the Negro Race, who through centuries, in his parents and grandsires, had helped make him what he is."[120] Crummell was determined not to let the new black leadership lose the traditions of the black race with assimilationist doctrines.

No single concern dominated Crummell's later life more than this faith in the masses. In a private letter, he had responded to Hoffman's racist claims of the biological and moral inferiority of the masses of black people: "Fully one-third of our people are growing up virtuously, industrially, religiously, and monetarily."[121] The letter further suggested that there was another one-third of the black population at a "standstill" but ready to be motivated upwards. He genuinely believed that there was a latent genius "garnered up in the by-places and sequestered corners of this neglected race,"[122] and on his death bed, he expressed an undying faith in the Negro race though he did feel apprehensive about its leaders: "I have no fear of the future of the American Negro, for he belongs to a prolific, hardy and initiative race, and there is a glorious future before him; but I do dread his leaders, because most of them are unscrupulous, ambitious and ungodly men, who care nothing for the race."[123] On the one hand, he rejected the idea of dilettantes, "fools . . . who imitate the style and fashion of 5th Avenue millionaires,"[124] assuming leadership roles; on the other hand, he warned against breeding a class of snobbish "superscholars" who craved for the limelight. Instead, the race needed intellectuals who would willingly "work . . . in the shade," finding it reward enough to know that they had offered their learning and vision "to serve a benighted and struggling Race."

BLACK EDUCATION

Though he had expressed to Bruce an unwilling-
ness to come forward as the new leader, Crummell
did assert leadership in black education. During the
1880s, while he was pleading the cause of
dispossessed Blacks and had begun probing the
difficult question of black leadership, he also
addressed the perennial problem of black education.
He envisioned an educational program that would
give poor Blacks employable skills and prepare prospective black leaders for a life of service to their
race. Such an educational policy geared to self-
development became increasingly important in
Crummell's Pan-African ideal.

"Culture is a great need," Crummell admitted,
"but the greater, wider need of the race is industry
and practicality."[125] He urged black parents to see
to it that their children attended trade schools and
qualified as productive artisans. Directing his
attention to the wretched of the race, he
recommended that one large industrial school be
established in every Southern state for the training of
black girls of the South. It was a revolutionary
recommendation in that it went beyond domestic
training and called for instruction in reading, writing,
arithmetic, and geography.[126] In Liberia, Crummell
had displayed this perceptive and avant-garde vision
in respect to black women, for he had advocated the
education of African girls and women and advised the
Mission Board to send twice as many women
missionaries as men.[127] Crummell was deliberately
pitting an industrial school for the forgotten
"plantation women," against a Spelman College which
was opened recently for "upper status" Negro women.
Defending practical and utilitarian training against a
more academic and classical curriculum, Crummell
contended that "utility is the grander, for it is the
necessary, nay the absolute, object of our being."[128]

Paul Laurence Dunbar expressed a particular liking for Crummell's strong appeal for industrial training and praised him for displaying "conservative common sense and an intelligent perception of the needs and shortcomings of our race."[129] Also, Crummell's focus on industrial education did seem to endorse Booker T. Washington's political program as expressed in 1884: "Good school teachers and plenty of money to pay them will be more potent in settling the race question than any civil rights bill."[130]

Crummell was running into the old problem of imbalance. In an 1881 address, "The Dignity of Labor," he had encouraged the masses newly emerging from slavery to find dignity in servile and menial labor. He knew he was treading on dangerous ground, for white America would be only too anxious to relegate the black race to the caste of servitude. Thus, after having observed the virtues of domestic service, he remonstrated, "We must resist the attempt to make us a caste of servants in the land."[131]

So, too, the industrial training that he had encouraged was becoming the only avenue of education open to black people. Booker T. Washington had taken the industrial approach to education to an extreme level, and Crummell disagreed vehemently: "To allege industrialism to be the grand agency in the elevation of a race of already degraded laborers, is as much a mere platitude as to say, 'they must eat and drink and sleep.'"[132] Crummell was sharpening the scythe with which Du Bois was later to sweep away the dominance of Washington's philosophy of education. Crummell ridiculed the notion that the Negro must start at the bottom not at the top, "as though the Negro had been living in the clouds" and needed to be called, for the first time, "to blister his hands with the hoe, and to learn to supply his needs by sweatful toil in the cotton fields."[133] He was warning lest, in the great anxiety to produce skilled laborers who would be able to fit well into the modern industrial age, the black race might become mere thoughtless toilers, a race of "senseless *boys*." He knew that only thinking people were men, and he exhorted the black laboring class to bring thought to their labor and to demand a larger share of the wealth their labor brought to others. "Do not use your labor to make the white man a Croesus," he warned.

The truth is, at no time in his career had Crummell ever abandoned his Talented Tenth theory. Even in his 1886 "Common Sense in Common Schooling" address, in which he advocated practical, utilitarian training in the trades, he admitted the need for a "class of trained and superior men and women." He later defined these "fit and exceptional cases" to be minds able to "grasp ideal truth."[134] Even in his stirring oration, "The Black Woman of the South," he enthusiastically supported institutions like Spelman College. Actually, two years before "Common Sense," at a high school in Washington, D.C., Crummell presented an address entitled, "Excellence, an End of the Trained Intellect," in which he focused on the virtues of a classical training. These addresses anticipated both sides of the celebrated Du Bois—Washington debate over the "proper" educational pathway for black America. It is important to stress that Crummell, like Du Bois and Washington, acknowledged the value and importance of both kinds of education for the proper development of the race. Nonetheless, the fact was that Booker T. Washington's emphasis on trade-training was gaining acceptance as the direction which black education ought to follow.

Firm in his belief of an elite leadership class, and urged on, no doubt, by young Blacks like John Bruce to take a leadership role in the black community, Crummell began organizing in the early 1890s an African institute. William Ferris, a contemporary and personal friend of Crummell's, claimed that an institute for black intellectuals was a dream that Crummell first had while he was a student at Cambridge University.[135] Crummell might have had such a dream, but the actual plan to found the American Negro Academy (ANA) came to Crummell from William H. Crogman on the advice of the Reverend Francis J. Grimké.[136] Grimké was a Presbyterian minister who became treasurer of the academy for the first twenty-two years of the life of the organization. Crogman was a professor of the classics at Clark University, Atlanta.

Once the plan was agreed upon, Crummell became the organizing force. Significantly, the title which he had suggested for the organization at the first planning meeting was "the African Academy." The term African carried with it the race-designation central to his Pan-African ideas. He drew up the constitution for the proposed academy, in which he stated five goals, all of which emphasized the promotion of black culture, and limited the number of members to forty. Members were required to be either "graduates or Professors in Colleges . . . [or] Authors, Artists, and distinguished writers."[137] Though the racial description of these authors, scholars, and artists was "colored," Crummell was happy to write to Bruce that at one of their meetings, "every speaker was a Negro, pure and unadulterated."[138] Also, when a light-skinned black person, Richard Theodore Greener, a graduate of Harvard College and a former dean of Howard University's law school, applied for membership to the academy, Crummell vigorously opposed his admission on grounds that Greener, he believed, "passed for white when it suited him."[139] Though three of the five goals included in the constitution proposed publication of scholarly works, Crummell was determined that his scholarly organization never forget that it was black. So well did he convey this "race feeling" toward the organization, several years after his death, his friend Bruce, bewailing the mulatto leadership of the academy, demanded the election of a leader who was a "black scholar soaked from his toes to the outer surfaces of his caput in the ideas . . . which Dr. Crummell held."[140]

The four other members at the planning meeting of the organization decided on the title, "The American Negro Academy." Other prospective members were invited, and Crummell was elected chairman of the organizational meetings. As the academy became more firmly established, he was persuaded by W.E.B. Du Bois and others to accept the post of president, and he was unanimously elected. He remained president for eighteen months until his death.

During his tenure as president of the ANA, Crummell saw his ideas and efforts extended through young black intellectuals. The first publication of the academy was Kelly Miller's *Review of Hoffman's Race Traits and Tendencies of the American Negro* (1897) which fell in line with Crummell's address in England that refuted white racists' claims of superiority, and with his defense of the black race against the scurrilous attacks of Tucker. The second publication of the ANA, Du Bois's *The Conservation of the Races*, also supported Crummell's position that the black race had unique characteristics which needed to be preserved and shared for the benefit and development of mankind. The ANA, under Crummell, was providing the kind of Talented Tenth leadership that was healthy and profitable for the black race as a whole. Moreover, news of the ANA's existence reached Crummell's West Indian and African friends in England, who, in turn, established the Central British African Association.[141] Under Crummell, the ANA could well be considered the first step towards a Pan-African organization, for it was the leadership of the Central British African Association that called the first Pan-African Conference.

The establishment of the American Negro Academy, Crummell's last great achievement, was a significant shift from the emphasis he had placed on the black masses during the past twenty–five years of his life. But he had by no means abandoned the downtrodden class, for it was in the inaugural address to the academy that he encouraged the scholars to draw forth the latent genius of the race, "garnered up . . . in sequestered corners." The ANA signified a keener awareness on Crummell's part that the improved physical welfare of the masses by itself could not bring about the uplift of the black race.

"The [race] battle in America is to be carried on in the world of the minds," he had written Professor J. W. Cromwell,[142] and the establishment of the Negro Academy was his contribution to this struggle. After attending Queen Victoria's Diamond Jubilee in England in 1897, Crummell, an old man and ailing, repeated in a letter to a friend that the black man had a fight for his mind facing him: "I am inclined to think that we have a severe battle before us."[143] The following year, he reasserted to the Reverend Frazier Miller: "The problem in the U.S.A. is a problem of ideas."[144]

The change from stressing as his primary concern the physical well–being of the black race was not difficult to make, for Crummell had never forgotten that "we are all God's property . . . for [his] service and his praise."[145] When he had encouraged black industry, he grounded his appeal on the spiritual conviction that "to work is a law of existence with God, Angels, and with men."[146] So, too, black education "should reach for excellence, not so much for itself, as for the facile use of powers it gives us in the duties of life."[147] In social concerns, he preached that "the true grandeur of a people is not to be found in their civil status, [nor] in their political franchises,"[148] and so he enjoined the Storer College graduating class to forget themselves and "live for the good of man and the glory of God."[149]

Crummell's eyes were ever fixed on the invisible world. In 1890, he appealed to the St. Thomas Church audience to "be ever mindful of the reality of the invisible world; of the presence of Divine and heavenly things amid temporal concerns and earthly relations."[150] In this same address, he referred to "a higher groove of existence" and "the domain of the spirit world."[151] In these phrases, Crummell expressed his deep conviction that man had the capacity of living on a higher plane of existence, in a world that was not comparable to this physical world of phenomena, far from "the crazy rush of madding crowd." It was the possibility of this expanded consciousness that Crummell was always holding before his listeners, especially in the later years of his life. Confident that there was a divine and all–powerful energy that shaped man's history, an energy that permeated the entire universe, Crummell with undying optimism believed that, in the end, "all the shadows and mist which obscure our vision shall vanish away."[152] Thus, before the Garnet Lyceum, he had assured the Lincoln University students that if they dedicated their lives to the grand themes of life—the soul of man, the grand moral entities, and the great unsettled questions of the spirit—they would experience "a light which never streamed from stars or sun; and a power [would] come into [their] innermost being, fitting [them] for the grandest purpose of existence."[153] Crummell was obviously referring, from personal experience, to the spiritual vision he had cultivated as a boy and had nurtured throughout his adult life. He had learned that all real success in life sprang from inward might, and so he warned that "neither science . . . nor learning . . . nor erudition . . . nor observation . . . can suffice for that inward spirit of intelligence." This spiritual faculty in man which Crummell always tried to encourage men to cultivate was the "one great commanding central quality" that resided behind the physical, mental, and moral qualities in man. For man to properly develop the spiritual capacity in himself, he must learn "to possess himself."[154] The possession of self ran along lines similar to "possession of one's race-harmony." Even as he warned that a race had to restrain its natural bent and counterbalance its tendency with complementary characteristics not peculiar to the race, so must an individual guard against the absorbing self-concentration of any single faculty. In directing his listeners in the ways of spiritual growth, he instructed: "The harmonious development of your capacities is the surest means for the attainment of that inward magistracy and rule."[155] The harmonious development of man was the pathway for the evolution of the spiritual quality with which each man was endowed. The world of the senses was real and important, but it must not dominate man's existence. Man, like the butterfly, must transcend his fleshly caterpillar state and fly above the earth; only then would he live up to his capabilities. As Crummell put it: "If we are content with the earthly and the carnal, if we are engrossed with the sensible and material, then we shall surely eschew the heavens above."[156] Man must not deny his senses but should go through them to the spiritual realm which dwelled within him. The balancing of the sensual self with the spiritual being was the very essence of a "right-minded" man in Crummell's eyes. Crummell insisted that right-mindedness was available to all men, even the humblest, for in all men's souls were the laws and principles that governed the harmonious development of men. Human nature expressed the universal nature, and so all the cosmic laws and facts of the universe were the common heritage of humanity. These laws and principles, however, abided in the realms of the mind and spirit, and man, therefore, had to develop that spiritual side of his nature if ever he hoped to fulfill all of his human possibilities. The progress of humanity, the destiny of the human race, lay in the cultivation of the spiritual faculty in all men. This belief in the spirit underpinned all of Crummell's thoughts throughout his life. In seeking to elevate the black race by enjoining black people to cultivate the "personal element which differences the abiding things from the merely factitious and ephemeral," Crummell had sought to elevate the entire human race.

Though he had become firmly committed to ameliorating the conditions of black people in America and to cultivating the spiritual vision in man, Crummell's international Pan-African vision was by no means obscured. As he aged and gradually was losing his sight to the extent that he had to hire an amanuensis to get out letters concerning his debts, his Pan-African dream remained foremost in his mind. Half-blind, he still kept up correspondence with black people in Africa, in the West Indies, and in England. In a letter to Francis J. Grimké, dated June 30, 1886, he complained, "My sight is going . . . [and] I have important letters from England, Africa, and the West Indies, unanswered in my drawers."[157] It was with these correspondents that he first shared his ideas for the establishment of the Negro Academy. To the very end, his interest in Africa and the black man was keen. A few days before his death, on hearing of the fall of Khartoum, he was reported to have raised his hands and exclaimed: "Thank God! That marks the downfall of slavery in Central Africa."[158] And writing to Professor Cromwell the year before his death, Crummell decried the black American leaders who seemed to be working for individual power and personal fame instead of for the development of the black race: "The difference between the African and West Indian black man versus the American black man seems to be *this*—the *former* works and writes for his *race*, the latter for politics and an office."[159] Crummell had overstated his case, for surely the problem of caste is a problem of all Blacks in the New World—the United States, the Caribbean, and South America. Indeed, privilege according to a subtly defined hierarchy of color has permeated the Caribbean islands, and devotion to race is not only discouraged but outrightly condemned by most of the colored middle class in the West Indian nations. However, Crummell's impatience with his color-struck Afro–American brothers was quite understandable, for his West Indian and African associates were generally those who had shared devotion to the African race. Two decades later, when Afro–American intellectuals accused Garvey of importing the "West Indian mulatto problem" into the black American com-munity, they were misplacing their attacks, and like Crummell before them, they were wrongly imputing a New World black problem to national boundaries. Even today, in the 1980s, the color problem is a real problem among black people in America, in the Caribbean, in South America, and in some of the westernized nations in Africa. Alexander Crummell and Edward Blyden were two outstanding nineteenth–century black intellectuals who squarely had confronted this problem of color, and in the twentieth century, Marcus Garvey also challenged this doctrine of caste espoused by many colored New World Blacks. One of the finest treatments of the impotence of the half–black man when he yearns to hold on to his white blood and reject his black her-itage can be found in Vic Reid's *The Leopard*. This Jamaican novelist painted the half–bwana, who toadied after the white man's ways and scorned his African traditions, as a burden both to the white man and the black man. It is important to note that Garvey, Blyden, Crummell, and Reid expressed con-tempt for a particular kind of black man, the kind who puts a premium on the white blood that courses through his veins and feels shame and even scorn for his black strain. Crummell certainly did not seek to create an unbridgeable breach between the coloreds and the blacks; as he himself put it in his Jubilate address, "My heart, from youth, was consecrated to my race and its interests."

Crummell's Pan–African dream was based on his belief that all races possessed characteristics inherently and innately peculiar to them. Those characteristics, however, could be shared by the entire human family, only that each particular race had the tendency and hence the responsibility for developing its peculiar characteristics. To the very last years of his life, Crummell kept delineating the special capacities of the black race. Addressing black students from Lincoln University, he had referred to the abiding quality of "race peculiarities," and in his 1885 Storer College address, he identified "aesthetical culture" as a special aptitude of the black race and noted that "we are still a tropical race" and tropical warmth could be found in black songs and in black people's love of color.[160] However, Crummell had warned that black people had to ignore the strongest bent of their nature and concentrate on the primal duties of a practical life. In his address before the Garnet Lyceum, Crummell again had underscored that tendency of the "love of the beautiful among our people," but he was much sterner in the need to rein in that natural bent. He castigated cultivated colored Americans for being too exclusively "aesthetical," and after acknowledging that in the mind of black people there was a "permanent *tropical* element," he went on to bewail the fact that nowhere could he find blacks pursuing the harder studies which demanded more scholarship as a counterbalance to that tendency to indulge in the arts.[161] Significantly, not only did Crummell acknowledge that all people have peculiar racial traits, but that those traits could be curbed and other qualities developed in order to create a more balanced people. Thus, in his 1890 address at the laying of the cornerstone of St. Thomas Church in Philadelphia, Pennsylvania, he had urged his audience to learn the "noble Discipline of Freedom" and take that newfound discipline to their brothers in the South and to the missions of the church on the coast of Africa. Clearly, then, peculiar racial traits were not intended to separate men into isolated racial groups but to give each race special gifts to bring to the entire human family. Consequently, each race had the responsibility of learning from the other races, so that no race would remain lopsidedly barbaric.

CRUMMELL'S FINAL DAYS

Never did Crummell hesitate to help his fellow man, especially his black brothers. And always that help sought to balance physical and practical assistance with inner growth. He felt the pride of a teacher who sees his pupils fare well, but what impressed him most was not the prominent positions they held in Sierra Leone, and Lagos; not the fact that some had become wealthy merchants, others teachers and ministers, yet another a professor, one the secretary of state for Liberia, another an editor, and one even a bishop; what impressed Crummell most was the "superior life and character" he noticed in the letters they had written to him.[162] He liked recalling how a former pupil of his who had become secretary of state for Liberia remembered Crummell as being "a little too rigid." That reputation Crummell liked, for he felt that moral rigidity was a great need for a people in their passage from slavery to freedom. In recounting his contributions to the Liberian nation, Crummell would proudly proclaim, "I tolerated no iniquity, and . . . I rebuked depravity."[163] On a more personal level, he offered assistance to Paul Laurence Dunbar. He advised

Dunbar to live in Washington, D.C. and encouraged him to edit a magazine for black literature, reviews, and other literary topics.[164] Also, it was recorded that within a few hours of his death he dictated a letter to Dunbar on the philosophy of poetry. Unfortunately, no traces of this letter could be located. Crummell's selflessness and devotion to helping others was as much a part of the man as his intellectual brilliance. Two weeks before he died, he felt the mantle of death about to enshroud him and carefully arranged his own funeral. That detail being settled, the Reverend Matthew Anderson writes, "He at once seemed to be forgetful of all further thought of self, but to be concerned principally about the welfare of his race."[165] In fact, the last year of Crummell's life was not characterized by well-deserved rest but was filled with arduous labor as he strove to better the conditions of his race. He wrote to John Bruce: "I work daily six to eleven hours at my desk when I am able to write. But time tells on me, and at times I have to sit and do nothing and wait upon the Lord."[166] In 1897, he had written to Bruce, "I shan't be surprised if you laugh in your sleeve at an old man, nigh four score, projecting new work. I can't help it. Work is life."[167] The work to which Crummell was referring was the founding of the academy to register his protest against relegating the black race to menial labor. As for the spiritual uplift of the race, there is, among the John W. Cromwell family papers, a letter from the publisher, Thomas Whittaker, that as late as July 12, 1898, Crummell was trying to get a book of sermons published.

While Crummell lay on his bed dying, his devoted wife, Jennie, attended him. A week before his death, she wrote to Professor Cromwell, "No decided change in the Doctor's condition,"[168] and at 10:30 a.m. September 10, 1898, Crummell died holding the hand of his faithful wife. The last moments before his death were devoted to prayer, conducted by his faithful spiritual advisor, a Father Wood. He had joined in the praying and singing of the morning devotion and passed away to be numbered, undoubtedly, among the just.

The passing of Crummell was the passing of a significant African presence in the New World. No mention was made of any of his children being present at his funeral, but his brother Charles and Sidney's wife did attend the final services.[169] Crummell had served his race better than he had attended his family. The newspapers reported the passing away of this great black man. The Pittsburgh *Herald* wrote: "As the prophets and great men of old are still speaking to us and influencing us through their writings, so will Dr. Crummell continue to do. . . . He had a brilliant imagination. . . . Blood will tell. Dr. Crummell was the grandson of a king. He was a born ruler. . . . He was no trimmer; he could not cringe."[170] The Washington *Post* in an obituary column on September 11, 1898, described him as being "easily one of the finest scholars of his times." The Reverend Henry Phillips in his *In Memoriam* address, proclaimed as an epitaph: "The life, the hardships, the struggles of a man like Dr. Crummell should be known and studied by all the youths of the country."[171] Professor Ferris, who knew Crummell personally, perhaps presented the best and fullest physical description of Crummell:

Tall, slender, symmetrical, erect in bearing, with a graceful and elastic walk, with a refined and aristocratic face that was lighted up by keen penetrating but kindly eyes, and surrounded by the grey hair and beard which gave him a venerable appearance, with a rich, ringing, resonant baritone voice, which had not lost its power even in old age, with an air of unmistakable good breeding and a conversation that flavored of books and

literature and art, Dr. Crummell was a man
that you could never forget, once you met
him or heard him preach.[172]

In many respects, Crummell was one of the grandest
characters of the black race to have lived during the
nineteenth century. He has been described variously
as "the Sir Philip Sidney of the race," as the "Nestor
of his people," "as the Newman of the Negro pulpit,"
but the finest homage paid Crummell was by his
protégé, W.E.B. Du Bois who, in 1899, read "Strivings
of a Negro for the Higher Life" at a Tuskegee
Institute meeting. Professor William James, the
noted American philosopher, who was a member of
the audience, doubted that there ever was such a real
Crummell. This eulogy was later published as "Of
Alexander Crummell" in the epoch-making *The Souls
of Black Folk*. Du Bois wrote of his first meeting with
Crummell, "Instinctively I bowed before this man, as
one bows before the prophets of the world. Some seer
he seemed."[173] Du Bois had recognized the spiritual
nature of this great man, and he mourned the fact
that his name meant so little across the length and
breadth of America: "In another age he might have
sat among the elders of the land in purple-bordered
toga; in another country mothers might have sung
him to the cradles."[174]

Epilogue

Crummell's life spanned almost the entire nineteenth century and was distinguished by intellectual achievements and missionary work: but his was not a blameless life. There were some who found his lifestyle unbearable. His family, for example, could not always endure him. Crummell expected his wife and children to live the same rigorous and ascetic life he lived. He did not seem to realize that almost his entire youthful life was a preparation for the kind of selfless and self-mortifying life he demanded of his family. His struggles at Canaan, New Hampshire, his trying experiences with Bishop Onderdonk, his saintly living at Oneida Institute, helped to form the ascetic character of Crummell. His first wife endured much with Crummell, but finally she had to divorce him. His daughters were not there to support him in his old age, and his son, Sidney, refused to attend his funeral.

Others who had close dealings with Crummell found him too fastidious and uncompromising on certain principles. His fellow black ministers in Liberia, his vestrymen at St. Luke's in the District of Columbia, and the young native African who sought to court Crummell's daughter without going through the proper channels, all found Crummell an intolerable stuffed shirt. So, too, Crummell's authoritative and almost autocratic manner in his racial beliefs made him unbearable in the eyes of people like Bishop Payne in Liberia, and T. Thomas Fortune in the United States. Also, there was often a tone of self-righteous pride in the attacks Crummell made on the immoral characters of his antagonists; not even his son escaped his condemnation.

Significantly, however, Crummell never had enemies among the poor, the downtrodden, the oppressed. They were always willing to sign petitions, with X's if need be, in support of their pastor. Crummell was a champion of the wretched of the earth. His address, "The Black Woman of the South," epitomizes his compassionate concern for the plight of the poor.

Intellectuals and influential persons also had great respect and admiration for the Reverend Dr. Alexander Crummell. Frederick Douglass, William Wells Brown, Henry Highland Garnet, James McCune Smith, Edward Blyden, John W. Crommell, Francis J. Grimké, Daniel Payne, John E. Bruce, W.E.B. Du Bois and many other outstanding nineteenth-century black leaders acknowledged the greatness of Alexander Crummell. Even his antagonists, especially Bishop Payne, Sidney, and the vestrymen, admitted the piety and intellectual acumen of Dr. Crummell. T. Thomas Fortune, who at first challenged Crummell's intense race-conscious approach to the black man's problems, later seemed to subscribe to Crummell's racial doctrine for he (Fortune) eventually became editor of Marcus Garvey's *Negro World*.

Soon after Crummell's death, St. Luke's established an Alexander Crummell Fund, the money from which was used to build a Crummell Memorial. In the District of Columbia an elementary school was named after Crummell, and his name is still revered by D.C. residents who know about him.

Crummell was great, not in the sense that he changed the way of thought for succeeding generations, but in the way that he elaborated upon and made his own, the deep Christian faith that guided his life. There is no Sermon on the Mount in Crummell's life, a sermon in which he broke new ground and proclaimed, "In the past it was said . . . but I say to you . . ." Crummell accepted uncritically the beliefs of his age, and he preached that Christian "civilization" was the only hope for freeing Africa from its "dark and ignorant practices." But even given this serious limitation, Crummell always saw worth and wisdom in the unschooled ways of the native African. More importantly, Crummell always believed that Africa was once great, and he often suggested that the problem of the age was to uncover the grandeur that was once Africa's. He was convinced that Christianity was the key for uncovering the past.

Today, more than eighty years since Crummell's death, his influence can be felt. His ideas on Pan-Africanism still pertain to the problems facing black people in America, in the Caribbean, in Latin America, in Europe, and in Africa. Were Crummell alive when Sylvester Williams called the first Pan-African Conference in 1900, most likely Crummell, instead of his protégé W.E.B. Du Bois, would have presided. The resurgence of scholarly interest in Africa's past is undoubtedly a legacy of the American Negro Academy. Walter Williams, who has been close to the work of Crummell, asserts that "Dr. Crummell was [the] instigator of the idea of collecting and studying works on the Negro," and thanks to Crummell, we have today the Moorland–Spingarn and Schomburg collections. Recent studies by black scholars such as Chancellor Williams of the United States, Cheik Anton Diop of Africa, and Ivan Van Sertima of the Caribbean, clearly follow the intellectual interest in Africa that Crummell encouraged in the last years of his life. Crummell's Pan-Africanism is becoming a reality on the level of scholarly research on Africa's past.

In the area of spiritual growth, Crummell's ideas about the ever-present invisible world have not made a significant mark on the black world. Black people have to concern themselves with technology and the business of practical affairs, and Crummell would agree with this deep concern. However, just as he saw no conflict between higher education and industrial education, he would today see no conflict between computer technology and spiritual energy, between electronics and prayer. Indeed, he would probe to see the underlying principle that would make the one complement the other.

But even if Crummell's ideas on black sociological research, on black education, on black solidarity had not left their mark on the modern black world, the example of his morally courageous life and his uncompromising commitment to Africa could be a significant influence for young black people. The Reverend Henry Phillips in his eulogy quite rightly asserted: "The life, the hardships, the struggles of a man like Dr. Crummell should be known and studied by all the youths of the country." However, important as Crummell's moral courage was, his devotion to Africa characterizes him even better. Five months before he died, Crummell revealed to John Bruce that Henry Highland Garnet never used the term "farewell" as his parting remark in letters. Garnet had coined his own parting phrase: "Africa forever." Garnet's phrase is a fitting epitaph for Crummell.

Notes

PROLOGUE

1. W.E.B. Du Bois, *The Souls of Black Folk* (1903; Greenwich, Conn.: Fawcett Publications, Inc., 1961) 164–165.
2. See, for example, Wilson Moses, *The Golden Age of Black Nationalism, 1850–1925* (Hamden, Conn.: The Shoe String Press, 1978) 59–82; Wilson Moses, "Alexander Crummell: Civilizing Missionary," *Journal of Negro History* 60 (April 1975) 229–251; August Meier, *Negro Thought in America 1880–1915* (Ann Arbor: University of Michigan Press, 1963) 42–43. Vernon Loggins, *The Negro Author* (1931; Port Washington, New York: Kennikat Press, 1964) 199–209; Kathleen O. Whale, "Alexander Crummell: Black Evangelist and Pan-Negro Nationalist," *Phylon* 29 (Winter 1968) 388–395; Monday Benson Akpan, "Alexander Crummell and His African 'RaceWork': An Assessment of His Contributions in Liberia to Africa's 'Redemption,' 1853–1873," *Historical Magazine of the Protestant Episcopal Church* 46 (June 1977) 177–199.
3. There have been a few biographical works on Crummell: Henry Phillips, *In Memoriam of the Late Reverend Alexander Crummell* (Philadel-

phia: Coleman, 1899); William Henry Ferris, *Alexander Crummell, an Apostle of Negro Culture* (Washington, D.C.: American Negro Academy, 1920); Ronald N. Fox, "The Reverend Alexander Crummell: An Apostle of Black Culture" (unpublished B.S.T. thesis, General Theological Seminary, 1969); Otey M. Scruggs, *We the Children of Africa in This Land: Alexander Crummell* (Washington, D.C.: Howard University Press, 1972).
4. See John H. Bracey, Jr., August Meier, and Elliott Rudwick, eds., *Black Nationalism in America* (New York: The Bobbs–Merrill Company, Inc., 1970) xxvi–xxx.

CHAPTER 1

1. *Alexander Crummell Papers*, Schomburg Collection, Harlem Branch of the New York Public Library, "Africa and Her People." Hereafter, *A.C. Papers*. For a somewhat dramatized version of Boston Crummell's capture, auction block experiences in the West Indies, enslavement in the United States, and subsequent escape from slavery, see Walter B. Hayson's eulogy on Alexander Crummell delivered before the American Negro Academy, Dec. 27–28, 1898, in *The Church Standard*, 14 Jan. 1899: 355.
2. Phillips, *In Memoriam*, 10.
3. Vernon R. Dorjahn, "The Changing Political System of the Temne," *Africa* 30 (April 1960) 109–140.
4. Alexander Crummell, *The Shades and Lights of a Fifty Year's Ministry* (Washington, D.C.: R.L. Pendleton, 1894) 7. Hereafter, Jubilate.
5. Alexander Crummell, "The Black Woman of the South" in *Africa and America* (1891; New York: Negro University Press, 1969) 79.

6. *John E. Bruce Papers*, Schomburg Collection, Harlem Branch of the New York Public Library, New York. Letter dated Jan. 1894.
7. "The Black Woman of the South" 71.
8. See Ferris, *Apostle of Negro Culture*, and Phillips, *In Memoriam*.
9. Daniel A. Payne, *Recollections of Seventy Years* (1891; New York: Arno Press, Inc., 1968) 42.
10. This address marked the formal entry of the American black man into the abolition movement. White "gentlemen" had to attest to the authenticity of this speech being Williams's composition. See Dorothy Porter's *Early Negro Writing* (Boston: Beacon Press, 1971).
11. Williams, "Abolition of the Slave Trade" in Porter's *Early Negro Writing* 345.
12. "Abolition of the Slave Trade" 349.
13. In 1815, Paul Cuffe, a self-trained black entrepreneur who owned and navigated his own sea vessels, had settled thirty-eight black Americans in Sierra Leone, West Africa, at considerable personal expense. Cuffe had expressed interest in an African colonization plan. See Floyd Miller, *The Search for a Black Nationality: Black Emigration and Colonization* (Urbana: University of Illinois Press, 1975) 21–53.
14. Miller, *Black Nationality* 43. See also Henry N. Sherwood, "Paul Cuffe," *Journal of Negro History* 8 (April 1923) 204.
15. Sherwood, "Paul Cuffe" 207. Correspondence between Peter Williams, Jr., and Cuffe can be found in Sheldon H. Harris, *Paul Cuffe: Black America and the African Return* (New York: Simon and Schuster, 1972), chapter 4.
16. Peter Williams, Jr., *Discourse Delivered on the Death of Captain Paul Cuffe* (New York: B. Young and Co., 1817) 16.
17. Peter Williams, Jr., "A Discourse Delivered in St. Phillips Church, for the Benefit of the

Coloured Community of Wilberforce, in Upper Canada," in Porter's *Early Negro Writing* 301.

18. *Discourse on the Death of Cuffe* 13.
19. *Discourse on the Death of Cuffe* 13.
20. *Discourse on the Death of Cuffe* 15.
21. James McCune Smith, "Introduction" to Henry Highland Garnet's *A Memorial Discourse* (Philadelphia, 1865) 24.
22. Howard Bell, ed., *Minutes of the Proceedings of the National Negro Conventions, 1830–1864* (New York: Arno Press, Inc., 1969), "1835 Convention" 14–15.
23. See, for example, Mary Thompson's *The Colored Home in the City of New York* (New York: John F. Trow, 1851) passim.
24. P.J. Staudenraus, *The African Colonization Movement, 1816–1865* (New York: Columbia University Press, 1961) 48.
25. For a summary of black resistance to the ACS, see Leon Litwack, *North of Slavery* (Chicago: The University of Chicago Press, 1966) 24–28. See also Miller, *Black Nationality* 48–49, 54–55.
26. *Discourse on the Death of Paul Cuffe* 16.
27. "Discourse in St. Phillip's Church" 296.
28. "Abolition of the Slave Trade" 348.
29. "Discourse in St. Phillip's Church" 297.
30. "Discourse in St. Phillip's Church" 297.
31. Peter Williams, Jr., "Address Before the Phoenix Society," as reported in *Emancipator* 29 April 1834.
32. "Discourse in St. Phillip's Church" 296.
33. Russwurm was a graduate of Bowdoin University, Brunswick, Maine, on Sept. 6, 1826. Actually, the first black graduate, as Philip Foner has discovered, was Edward Jones, who received his degree from Amherst College on Aug. 23, 1826. See Philip Foner, ed., *The Voice of Black America*, (New York: Capricorn Books, 1975) 33.

34. *Freedom's Journal* 4 April 1827.
35. *Freedom's Journal* 7 Sept. 1827: 102, column 1.
36. Cornish announced that he had resigned to take up the job as the first "agent" of the African Free School. It is claimed, however, that Cornish and Russwurm had parted company on the issue of colonization. Russwurm had declared that Africa was the only place where the black man could be free. See Bella Gross, *"Freedom's Journal," Journal of Negro History* 17 (July 1932) 241–286.
37. *The Ebony Handbook* (Chicago: Johnson Publishing Company, Inc., 1974) 420.
38. "Introduction" 20.
39. *Freedom's Journal* 28 March 1829, 410, column 3.
40. Alexander Crummell, "Eulogium on Henry Highland Garnet" in *Africa and America* 275–276.
41. Alexander Crummell, *Civilization the Primal Need of the Race* (Washington, D.C.: American Negro Academy, 1898) 11.
42. See Jubilate address.
43. Alexander Crummell, "The Relations and Duties of the Free Colored Men in America to Africa," *The Future of Africa*, 2d ed. (New York: Charles Scribner, 1862) 218.
44. "Relations and Duties" 257.
45. "Relations and Duties" 253.
46. The facts of this section come from Howard Bell's *Minutes.*
47. Herbert Aptheker, ed., *A Documentary History of the Negro People in the United States*, 2 vols. (Secaucus, New Jersey: Citadel Press, 1951) 1: 201.
48. See Bell's *Minutes*, esp. 4, 5, 7, 9, 10, 11, 13, 31–32.
49. "Introduction" 21.
50. Charles Andrews, *History of New York African Free Schools* (New York: M. Day, 1830) 11.
51. Carter G. Woodson, *Free Negro Heads of*

Families in the United States in 1860 (Washington, D.C.: The Association for the Study of Negro Life and History, Inc., 1925) li–liii.
52. *History of Free Schools* 7.
53. *History of Free Schools* 39.
54. *History of Free Schools* 60.
55. A.H. Payne, "The Negro in New York Prior to 1860," *The Howard Review* 1 (June 1923) 48.
56. "Introduction" 21.
57. "Introduction" 26.
58. "Introduction" 21.
59. William Yates, *Rights of Colored Men* (Philadelphia: Merrihew and Gunn, 1838) 55.
60. John W. Cromwell, *The Negro in American History* (Washington, D.C.: The American Negro Academy, 1914) 130.
61. "Eulogium on Garnet" 279.
62. "Eulogium on Garnet" 279.
63. "Eulogium on Garnet" 279.
64. *A.C. Papers*, "Eulogy on Sidney" 14.
65. "Eulogium on Garnet" 280.
66. It seems that Garnet did not have the means to attend this school immediately though subsequently he did attend and did graduate with honors from Oneida Institute. (See James McCune Smith's "Introduction.")
67. "Introduction" 26, 27.
68. Garnet had written to Crummell, in somewhat cryptic language, that his father, Mr. Boston Crummell, "is very much altered," and continued, "you will find things much altered when you come home." (*A.C. Papers*, May 13, 1837).
69. *A.C. Papers*, "Eulogy on Sidney" 28.
70. *A.C. Papers*, "Eulogy on Sidney" 30.
71. Jubilate 6.
72. George Moore was accused of rape and imprisoned in New Haven. *A.C. Papers*, May 13, 1837.
73. It is not quite clear in what year Crummell graduated from Oneida Institute. All of his

biographers pinpoint the year 1839. Most likely they got that date from Crummell himself who stated in his Jubilate address that after graduating from Oneida, he applied for admission to the General Theological Seminary in New York in 1839. This seems to be inaccurate, for there is evidence that Crummell was refused admission to the General Theological Seminary in February, 1838. (See *Colored American*, 17 Feb. 1838: 3, column 2.) It would seem that Crummell graduated from Oneida Institute in 1837, though there is a letter dated July 9, 1838, which refers to an "Institute" which Crummell was attending. In the first place, the school could have been the equivalent of a modern day three–year senior high school, and the training at the African Free School probably covered up to junior high school (15 years of age). Probably, too, after his rejection by the General Theological Seminary, Crummell entered some other "Institute" in Camden, New Jersey, for the letter was postmarked from that city. Since it is a fact Crummell was denied admittance in February 1838, and since one of the arguments brought against the seminary was that Crummell was a well–qualified candidate, it would seem that Crummell graduated from Oneida Institute in 1837.

74. Jubilate 7.
75. Jubilate 8. Walter Bragg claims that the immediate cause of Bishop Onderdonk's rejection of Crummell was that South Carolina had recently endowed the seminary with a $15,000 professor's chair, and Onderdonk did not want to offend the state. See George Bragg's *The First Negro Priest on Southern Soil* (Baltimore: The Church Advocate Print, 1909) 56. See also Litwack 202. The "one instance" in Africa most likely refers to one of the many 'run–ins' Crum-

mell had with the Rt. Rev. John Payne, the white Episcopal bishop in Liberia.

76. *Colored American*, 17 Feb. 1838: 3, column 2.
77. Some students had evidently formed a society of which Crummell seemed to be treasurer, for he was advised in a letter to keep the money from a broken lamp for the society. Also, Crummell's judgment in the matter of writing seemed to have been held high, certainly by his correspondent, for he requested Crummell to read and "throw together," as he saw fit, some bombastic prose which his correspondent had written in appreciation of Nature. Moreover, the letter reflected a further development of the severe and austere person Crummell was becoming, for his correspondent wrote with bubbling enthusiasm about "the coming six weeks" which would be spent in "quiet study and religion." (*A.C. Papers*, 9 July 1838).
78. *Colored American* 28 Sept. 1839: 3, column 2.
79. *Colored American* 28 Oct. 1839.
80. *Colored American* 7 Dec. 1839: 2, column 3.
81. *A.C. Papers* June, 1840(?). (Letter 148).
82. See *Historical Survey Inventory of Church Archives in Columbia: The Protestant Episcopal Church, Diocese of Washington* (Washington: n.p., 1940).
83. For this "manly protest," Bishop Theodore Holly, in his greetings sent from Haiti on the occasion of Crummell's Jubilate, declared the "the colored clergy . . . are under an everlasting debt of gratitude to [Crummell] for whatever recognition of our right status in the ministry of that church we may now enjoy." For the full text of Holly's greetings, see George F. Bragg's *The First Negro Priest on Southern Soil* 59–63.
84. C. Peter Ripley, ed., *The Black Abolitionist Papers*, 1 vol. to date (Chapel Hill: The University of North Carolina Press, 1985) 145.

85. *A.C. Papers* May 3, 1841.
86. Twenty–three of the twenty–seven pieces of writing are unpublished and part of the *A.C. Papers* located in the Schomburg Collection. The four published pieces are: a letter to the black newspaper, *Colored American* (7 Dec. 1839); his New York State Convention address, delivered in Aug. 1840; his famous "Eulogium on Thomas Clarkson," delivered on 26 Dec. 1846; and his "Address on Education" at the Negro National Convention in 1847.
87. Page numbers with an "S" preceding them interpolated in the text refer to the unpublished manuscript in the *A.C. Papers*.
88. *Anna J. Cooper Papers*, Manuscript Division, The Moorland–Spingarn Research Center, Howard University, Washington, D.C. Her autograph book.
89. W.E.B. Du Bois carried on this tradition while he was a student in Germany. See *The Autobiography of W.E.B. Du Bois* (New York: International Publishers Co., Inc., 1968) 170–171.
90. *Civilization the Primal Need of the Race* 6.
91. *Civilization the Primal Need of the Race* 6.
92. *Civilization the Primal Need of the Race* 7.
93. *Civilization the Primal Need of the Race* 6.
94. *Civilization the Primal Need of the Race* 7.
95. *Civilization the Primal Need of the Race* 5.
96. See *A.C. Papers*, "Treatise on Education" 25. Page numbers with an "E" preceding them interpolated in this section of the text refer to this work.
97. Alexander Crummell, "Storer Address" in *Africa and America* 13.
98. *Minutes of the National Convention of Colored Citizens* (New York: n.p., 1847) 33–37.
99. See *A.C. Papers*, "Sermons." The following quotations refer to the manuscript, "The Perfect Law of Liberty."

100. See *A. C. Papers*, "Sermons." Quotations following in this section of the text refer to this 1843 sermon.
101. See *A.C. Papers*, "Sermons." Quotations following in this section of the text refer to the sermon, "The Existence and Essence of God."
102. "The Perfect Law of Liberty" 11.
103. *A.C. Papers*, "Thy Kingdom Come." The page numbers in parentheses in the text refer to this sermon.
104. Ferris, *Apostle of Negro Culture* 6.
105. Crummell, "Eulogium on the Life and Character of Thomas Clarkson, Esq., of England" in *Africa and America*. The quotations in this section of the text refer to this work.

CHAPTER 2

1. *A.C. Papers*, "Letter" June 5, n.d. [1849]; also, report in *Record* newspaper, June 5, in *A.C. Papers*; and Frederick Douglass's *North Star*, 18 May 1849: 3, column 4. An account of the founding of the Church of the Messiah, along with thumbnail sketches of Peterson, DeGrasse and Jones, may be found in *Black Abolitionist Papers* 350–351, 352–353.
2. "The Perfect Law of Liberty."
3. Crummell was married and had five children. See *A.C. Papers*, Newspaper notice. Compare with C. Peter Ripley's editorial claim that Crummell had three children when he sailed for Liberia (*Black Abolitionist Papers* 147). Maybe the newspaper notice meant a family of five.
4. *A.C. Papers*, "Letter," 15 July 1845. While in England, Crummell, in a letter to John Jay, reiterated this offer to his wife and himself to further their education at English institutions at the expense of an unidentified lady in Bath and a Bath Committee (*Black Abolitionist*

Papers 146, 147).
5. Jubilate 10.
6. *A.C. Papers*, "Letter," 1848.
7. For a comprehensive survey of black Americans' visits to the British Isles between 1830 and 1865, see the introduction to *Black Abolitionist Papers* 3–35.
8. Julian D. Mason, ed., "Introduction" to *The Poems of Phillis Wheatley* (Chapel Hill: The University of North Carolina Press, 1966) xiv–xv.
9. George Shepperson, "Frederick Douglass and Scotland," *Journal of Negro History* 38 (July 1953) 308.
10. Benjamin Quarles in his "Ministers Without Portfolio," *Journal of Negro History* 39 (Jan. 1954) 30 ff., discusses the various visits of "colored agitators" who "paraded through the British Isles" in the twenty years preceding the Civil War. For the warm and kind treatment received by black ministers visting England in the postbellum period, see George F. Bragg, *The Episcopal Church and the Blackman* (Baltimore: n.p., 1918) 11.
11. William Wells Brown, *The American Fugitive in Europe* (Boston: J.B. Jewett and Company, 1855) 306.
12. Litwack 55.
13. As quoted in Litwack 249.
14. *North Star* 18 May 1849, 3, column 4.
15. *A.C. Papers*, See "Notice." For clarification of some misunderstandings concerning the disposition of the funds raised, see Crummell's letter to John Jay, 22 March, 1852 in *Black Abolitionist Papers* 308–310.
16. Jubilate 17.
17. *A.C. Papers*, See "Notice" concerning Cambridge University.
18. "Eulogium on Thomas Clarkson" 208.

19. "Eulogium on Thomas Clarkson" 208.
20. I am indebted to Mrs. Dorothy M. Owen, M.A., F.S.A., Keeper of the University of Cambridge Archives, for sending me a copy of the instructions for "The Previous Examination" of 1849.
21. Letter from Mrs. D.M. Owen.
22. *John W. Cromwell Family Papers*, Manuscript Division, The Moorland–Spingarn Research Center, Howard University, Washington, D.C. Letter dated Sept. 3, 1898.
23. *Civilization the Primal Need of the Race* 11.
24. *A.C. Papers, Record* newspaper, June 5.
25. *A.C. Papers, Record* newspaper, June 5. See also *Black Abolitionist Papers* 351.
26. *Future of Africa* 285.
27. *Future of Africa* 285.
28. *Future of Africa* 285.
29. Thomas Carlyle, *Critical and Miscellanous Essays*, Vol 4. of *Carlyle's Complete Works* (The Sterling Edition, n.d.), Vol. 16, 293–326.
30. *American Fugitive in Europe* 200. Carlyle later repeated his bitter opposition to the emancipation of the black man in *Shooting Niagara: And After* (1867): "The Almighty maker has appointed him [the black man] to be a Servant." (*Works*, Vol. 16, 425.).
31. *Future of Africa* 325–254.
32. *Future of Africa* 302.
33. *A.C. Papers*, Sermon 251.
34. This sermon was first preached at the Church of the Messiah in New York in October 1847, and was repeated eight times (twice in England and six times in Liberia). It was last preached in Liberia in 1873.
35. *Future of Africa* 302.
36. *Future of Africa* 312.
37. Jubilate 18.
38. *American Fugitive in Europe* 313.

39.   Jubilate 18.
40.   *American Fugitive in Europe* 313.
41.   *American Fugitive in Europe* 200.
42.   Eric Williams, *From Columbus to Castro: The History of the Caribbean 1492–1969* (New York: Harper & Row, Publishers, 1970) 319–320.
43.   Eric Williams, *Capitalism and Slavery* (New York: Capricorn Books Edition, 1966) 193.
44.   *Columbus to Castro* 405.
45.   J.J. Thomas, *Froudacity* (1889; London: New Beacon Books Ltd., 1969).
46.   *Capitalism and Slavery* 194–195.
47.   Alfred A. Moss, Jr., *The American Negro Academy*, (Baton Rouge: Louisiana State University Press, 1981) 54.
48.   Jubilate 17.
49.   *Domestic and Foreign Missionary Society: Liberia Records*, Archives of the Episcopal Church, Austin, Texas, letter March 22, 1865. Hereafter, *Liberia Records*.
50.   William Wells Brown, *The Black Man: His Antecedents, His Genius, and His Achievements* (New York: T. Hamilton, 1863) 169.
51.   *Liberia Records*, letter Oct. 1, 1852.
52.   *Liberia Records*, letter Feb. 10, 1853.

CHAPTER 3

1.   *Liberia Records*, letters April 22 and June 24, 1853.
2.   Alexander Crummell, "The Progress and Prospects of the Republic of Liberia" in *Future of Africa* 134.
3.   Alexander Crummell, "Address Before the Massachusetts Colonization Society," *African Repository* 37 (May 29, 1861) 280.
4.   *A.C. Papers*, "Africa and Her People," no. 23, n.d.

5. "Progress and Prospects" 92.
6. "Duty of a Rising Christian State" in *Future of Africa* 92.
7. "Duty of a Rising Christian State" 101.
8. "Duty of a Rising Christian State" 93.
9. "Duty of a Rising Christian State" 94.
10. *Liberia Records*, letter Aug. 8, 1853.
11. *Liberia Records*, letter Aug. 8, 1853.
12. *Liberia Records*, letter Oct. 4, 1853.
13. *Liberia Records*, letter Nov. 11, 1854.
14. *Liberia Records*, letter Feb. 12, 1856.
15. *Liberia Records*, letter April 15, 1857.
16. *Liberia Records*, letter May 4, 1857.
17. *Liberia Records*, letter March 8, 1865.
18. *Liberia Records*, "Seventeenth Annual Report of the Board of Managers of the Massachusetts Colonization Society," May 26, 1858.
19. *Liberia Records*, "Seventeenth Annual Report," May 26, 1858.
20. William Nesbit, *Four Months in Liberia* (Pittsburgh: J.T. Shryock, 1855) 43.
21. Samuel Williams, *A Sketch of the Life of the Reverend Samuel Williams* (Philadelphia: King and Baird, 1857) 59.
22. Williams 60.
23. Harriet G. Brittan, *Scenes and Incidents of Every-Day Life in Africa* (1860; New York: Negro University Press, 1969) 200–201.
24. Stanley Davis, *This is Liberia* (New York: The William Frederick Press, 1953) 102.
25. *Liberia Records*, letter Feb. 3, 1856.
26. *Liberia Records*, letter Dec. 8, 1853. For a pen-sketch of Stokes's life as a minister, see George Bragg, *The First Negro Priest on Southern Soil* 23–28.
27. *Liberia Records*, letter March 22, 1865.
28. Bishop Payne testified that Crummell had claimed that an influential clergyman in New York wanted him (Crummell) as bishop in

Liberia. *Liberia Records*, letter March 22, 1865.

29. *Liberia Records*, "Open Letter to Special Committee to Missions" (published Dec. 1864) 9.
30. *Liberia Records*, letter Aug. 8, 1853.
31. *Liberia Records*, letter March 28, 1854.
32. *Liberia Records*, letter "Semi-annual Report," April 1855.
33. *Liberia Records*, letter Aug. 26, 1854.
34. *Liberia Records*, letter Feb. 3, 1856.
35. *Liberia Records*, letter Nov. 11, 1854.
36. *Liberia Records*, letter March 28, 1854.
37. *A.C. Papers*, letter Nov. 4, 1863. On Sept. 8, 1865 he reiterated this opinion.
38. *Liberia Records*, "Open Letter to Special Committee to Missions" (published Dec. 1864) 9.
39. *Liberia Records*, "Bishop Payne's Correspondence, 1865–1866," March 22, 1865.
40. *Liberia Records*, letter March 8, 1865.
41. The Reverend Russell was not one of the black clergy who had signed the petition for an independent Liberian Church.
42. *Liberia Records*, letter March 8, 1865.
43. *Liberia Records*, letter May 7, 1866.
44. *Liberia Records*, letter May 7, 1866.
45. *Liberia Records*, letter Sept. 7, 1867.
46. *Liberia Records*, letter July 11, 1869.
47. *Liberia Records*, letter Feb. 1, 1869.
48. *Liberia Records*, letter June 10, 1869.
49. *Liberia Records*, "Bishop Payne's Correspondence" May 15, 1869.
50. *Liberia Records*, letter July 11, 1869.
51. *Liberia Records*, "Petitions in Crummell's Defense," Box 78.
52. *Liberia Records*, letter June 10, 1870.
53. *Liberia Records*, letter July 11, 1869.
54. W.F. Ferguson, a student at Liberia College, did make advances toward one of Crummell's daughters, and Crummell accused the young man of being "uncivilized" for not writing his

daughter through him. In a classic letter of sarcasm attacking Crummell's "superior attitude," Ferguson apologized: "I, a Liberian, can't know the proprieties of 'civilized countries.'" *A.C. Papers*, letter May 25, 1867.

55. *Liberia Records*, letter July 11, 1869.
56. *Liberia Records*, letter Nov. 20, 1870.
57. *Liberia Records*, letter Aug. 26, 1854.
58. Charles Foster, "The Colonization of Free Negroes in Liberia, 1816–1835," *Journal of Negro History* 38 (Jan. 1953) 41–66.
59. *Liberia Records*, letter May 7, 1866.
60. Hollis Lynch, *Edward Wilmot Blyden* (New York: Oxford University Press, 1967) 15.
61. Lynch, *Blyden* 15.
62. "Address Before the Massachusetts Colonization Society," *African Repository* 37 (May 29, 1861) 278–279.
63. Nesbit 42.
64. Samuel Williams 59.
65. Samuel Williams 16.
66. "God and the Nation" in *Future of Africa* 154.
67. *Liberia Records*, "Semi–Annual Report," April 1855.
68. "Relations and Duties" in 256, 246.
69. *Weekly Anglo–African* 27 April 1861.
70. "Relations and Duties" 256.
71. "Relations and Duties" 220.
72. "Relations and Duties" 258.
73. "Duty of a Rising Christian State" 63–64.
74. "Relations and Duties" 262.
75. "Relations and Duties" 218.
76. "Massachusetts Colonization Society," *African Repository* 277.
77. "Massachusetts Colonization Society," *African Repository* 278.
78. *African Repository*, letter Sept. 5, 1861, 312.
79. *African Repository*, letter Sept. 5, 1861, 311.
80. *African Repository*, letter Sept. 5, 1861, 312.

81. "Relations and Duties" 246.
82. "God and the Nation" 157.
83. "Address Before the American Geographical Society" in *Africa and America* 63.
84. "Duty of a Rising Christian State" 63.
85. "The English Language in Liberia" 10.
86. "The Fitness of the Gospel for Its Own Work" in *Future of Africa* 158.
87. *Liberia Records,* letter Sept. 9, 1870.
88. "The Fitness of the Gospel for Its Own Work" 188.
89. "Address on Laying the Corner-Stone of St. Mark's Hospital" in *Future of Africa* 208.
90. "God and the Nation" 152.
91. "God and the Nation" 166.
92. "Relations and Duties" 234.
93. *Liberia Records*, letter April 15, 1857.
94. "Address Before the American Geographical Society" 309–323. This address was sponsored by the African International Association.
95. "Address on Laying the Corner-Stone of St. Mark's Hospital" 206.
96. "Duty of a Rising Christian State" 74.
97. "Duty of a Rising Christian State" 74.
98. "Duty of a Rising Christian State" 65.
99. "Duty of a Rising Christian State" 97.
100. *Liberia Records*, letter Dec. 8, 1853.
101. *Liberia Records*, letter Oct. 4, 1853.
102. Lynch, *Blyden* 25.
103. *African Repository* 37 (April 1861) 98–99.
104. "Relations and Duties" 218.
105. "Relations and Duties" 216.
106. "Relations and Duties" 273.
107. "The English Language in Liberia" 12.
108. "Relations and Duties" 278.
109. "Relations and Duties" 249.
110. "Progress and Prospects" 148.
111. "Relations and Duties" 231.
112. "Relations and Duties" 245.

113. The full text of the address appeared in the Sept. 1861 edition of the *African Repository*.
114. "Address Before the Massachusetts Colonization Society," *African Repository*, Sept. 1861, 274.
115. "Relations and Duties" 218.
116. "The English Language in Liberia" 11.
117. "The Progress of Civilization Along the West Coast of Africa," *Future of Africa* 127.
118. "Massachusetts Colonization Society," *African Repository* 279.
119. "The Progress of Civilization" 127.
120. "Progress and Prospects" 147.
121. *Weekly Anglo-African*, 27 April 1861.
122. "Relations and Duties" 250.
123. *Weekly Anglo-African* 27 April 1861: 3.
124. "The Progress of Civilization" 127.
125. "Relations and Duties" 274.
126. "The English Language in Liberia" 9.
127. "The English Language in Liberia" 21.
128. "The English Language in Liberia" 26.
129. "The English Language in Liberia" 26.
130. "The English Language in Liberia" 27.
131. Edith Holden, *Blyden of Liberia* (New York: Vantage Press, Inc., 1966) 932. See also, *Minutes of the Massachusetts Colonization Society, May 28, 1862* 23. (4,000 volumes procured).
132. Litwack 278.
133. *Minutes of the Massachusetts Colonization Society* 28.
134. *American Colonization Society Papers*, Library of Congress, Washington, D.C., "Correspondence" 367.
135. Edwin S. Redkey, *Black Exodus: Black Nationalist and Back-to-Africa Movements, 1890-1910* (New Haven: Yale University Press, 1969) 38.
136. *Weekly Anglo-African*, 5 April 1862: 2.

137. *African Repository*, 38 (April 1862) 221.
138. *African Repository*, 38 (April 1862) 240.
139. Brittan 297.
140. "Progress and Prospects" 134.
141. *Liberia Records*, letter Jan. 31, 1872.
142. *Blyden* 40.
143. See Benedict Sekey's "A History of Liberia College" (Unpublished Master's Thesis, Howard University, 1973) 41.
144. Sekey 41.
145. Holden 83.
146. Holden 93.
147. *Blyden* 40.
148. Holden 92–93.
149. See *Minutes of Massachusetts Colonization Society*.
150. July 4, 1866, Volume 15 as quoted in Sekey 46–47.
151. Hollis Lynch, *Selected Letters of Edward Wilmot Blyden* (Millwood, New York: KTO Press, 1978) 55.
152. Sekey 45.
153. *Selected Letters* 322.
154. *Selected Letters* 340.
155. *Blyden* 47–48.
156. As quoted in *Blyden* 41, note 32.
157. *American Colonization Society Papers*, March 1866, as quoted in Feb. 11, 1867 letter 32.
158. *Selected Letters* 72–73.
159. One Mr. J.W. Duffin from New York City had proposed Crummell as rector of St. Phillip's in 1867. *A.C. Papers*, letter May 20, 1867.
160. *A.C. Papers*, letter from a Sierre Leone correspondent to Mrs. Crummell, Aug. 26, 1865.
161. *A.C. Papers*, letter Feb. 10, 1866.
162. *A.C. Papers*, letter Nov. 20, 1865. Morant Uprising.
163. *A.C. Papers*, letter Feb. 10, 1866.
164. *A.C. Papers*, letter Feb. 24, 1868.

165. *A.C. Papers*, letter Oct. 9, 1866.
166. *American Colonization Society Papers* 112.
167. *American Colonization Society Papers* 113.
168. *American Colonization Society Papers* 112.
169. *American Colonization Society Papers*, letter Oct. 30, 1867.
170. *American Colonization Society Papers*, letter July 31, 1868.
171. *American Colonization Society Papers*, letter July 31, 1868.
172. *Liberia Records*, letter June 10, 1868.
173. *American Colonization Society Papers*, letter Oct. 31, 1868.
174. *American Colonization Society Papers*, letter Oct. 31, 1868.
175. *American Colonization Society Papers*, letter Oct. 31, 1868.
176. *Liberia Records*, see 1868 Annual Report.
177. *American Colonization Society Papers*, letter June 16, 1869.
178. *Liberia Records*, letter Feb. 1, 1870.
179. *Blyden* 50–51.
180. *Blyden* 52–53.
181. *Selected Letters* 93–94.
182. *Selected Letters* 286.
183. *Blyden* 52.
184. *Selected Letters* 289–290.
185. *Blyden* 52–53.
186. *Selected Letters* 93.
187. As quoted in Redkey 230.
188. *Francis J. Grimké Papers*, Manuscript Division, The Moorland–Spingarn Research Center, Howard University, Washington, D.C.; folder 74, 1889.
189. *Francis J. Grimké Papers*, Folder 74, 1889.
190. Holden 47.
191. Holden 47.
192. *Liberia Records*, letter Feb. 21, 1871.
193. *Liberia Records*, letter Aug. 22, 1871.

194. See also, *American Colonization Society Papers*, Sept. 2, 1871, in which he wrote about a "melancholy crisis" and "a very dark four months before us." Crummell stressed that he wanted his letter to be kept "very private."
195. *Liberia Records*, letter Jan. 31, 1872.
196. In a letter to the secretary of the American Colonization Society, Crummell explained his personal goal: "the regeneration of the tribes around us." He went on to explain, "I shall see but little of the work done in my day; but I am anxious in my time to prepare a few men to commence it. So I eschew politics." *American Colonization Society Papers*, letter Nov. 6, 1871.

CHAPTER 4

1. *A.C. Papers*, Aug. 6, 1872.
2. *A.C. Papers*, Oct. 26, 1872. Crummell was, indeed, being considered to be the first black Episcopal bishop in the American Church. Bishop William Whittingham had expressed a willingness to vote for Crummell to be consecrated a bishop but he was not "prepared to nominate" him. (The Maryland Diocesan, on deposit at the Maryland Historical Society, Archives, Vertical File, May 27, 1872. Hereafter, M.D. Archives.) About one year later, Bishop Thomas Atkinson wrote: "As to a Bishop for the Freedmen . . . I should not be willing, certainly, to vote for . . . Crummell for that office." (M.D. Archives, July 1873). Crummell was never consecrated a bishop.
3. *A.C. Papers*, June 12, 1872.
4. *Blyden* 23.
5. *Blyden* 107.
6. M.D. Archives, Vertical File, Letter from The

Reverend John Vaughan Lewis to Bishop Whittingham, June 12, 1872.

7. It was a building formerly used by soldiers during the Civil War and placed on 23rd St., N.W.

8. M.D. Archives, Vertical File, July 25, 1872.

9. *A.C. Papers*, letter from John T. Johnson, D.C., Aug. 6, 1872.

10. *A.C. Papers*, letter from Gibson, Feb. 22, 1873.

11. M.D. Archives, Vertical File, letter from Crummell to Whittingham, June 13, 1873. Also, *A.C. Papers*, letter to Crummell, "You are the choice of your people as well as of the Bishop and Clergy." April 23, 1873.

12. M.D. Archives, Jan. 18, 1874.

13. M.D. Archives, Vertical File, July 12, 1876.

14. M.D. Archives, Vertical File, May 25, 1874.

15. *A.C. Papers*, June 18, 1873. Sidney himself had written to his father reporting that he was taking good care of his mother. However, in the same letter, Sidney revealed his 'dandy' character. He sent a photograph of himself for his father to show "girls in America," and he requested that his father, in turn, send him "half dozen or so" photographs of American girls. (*A.C. Papers*, n.d.).

16. *Black Abolitionist Papers* 145.

17. *Black Abolitionist Papers* 145.

18. *Black Abolitionist Papers* 144.

19. M.D. Archives, Bishop Whittingham's official *Journal*, 1874, 231.

20. M.D. Archives, Vertical File, Nov. 14, 1874.

21. See *St. Luke's Episcopal Church: One Hundred Years* (Washington, D.C.: The Church, 1973), especially Clotilda Barnett's essay (74–77) and Mary Price's interview with Miss Helen Moore (96).

22. "The Race–Problem in America" in *Africa and America* 48.

23.   "The Race-Problem in America" 53.
24.   Kenneth Stampp and Leon F. Litwack, eds., *Reconstruction: An Anthology of Revisionist Writings* (Baton Rouge: Louisiana State University Press, 1969) 15.
25.   "The Social Principle" in *The Greatness of Christ and Other Sermons* (New York: T. Whittaker, 1882) 287.
26.   See John H. Franklin's *Reconstruction After the Civil War* (Chicago: The University of Chicago Press, 1961); Benjamin Quarles's *The Negro in the Civil War* (Boston: Little, Brown and Co., 1953); and Rayford Logan's *The Negro in American Life and Thought: The Nadir, 1877–1901* (1954; published as *The Betrayal of the Negro, From Hayes to Wilson*, New York: Collier Books, 1965).
27.   "Social Principle" 299.
28.   M.D. Archives, Bishop Whittingham's Diary, Wed. Dec. 15, 1875.
29.   M.D. Archives, June 13, 1876.
30.   *St. Luke's Episcopal Church: One Hundred Years* 77.
31.   "Social Principle" 290.
32.   M.D. Archives, Vertical File, Sept. 13, 14, 1876.
33.   M.D. Archives, Vertical File, Jan. 11, 1877.
34.   M.D. Archives, Vertical File, Jan. 11, 1877. 1877 Convocation of Washington, Annual Report.
35.   *A.C. Papers*, "Opening Ceremony of St. Luke's Church, Washington, D.C.," Nov. 25, 1879.
36.   *St. Luke's Episcopal Church: One Hundred Years* 77.
37.   M.D. Archives, April 4, 1881. See also, letter from "Committee of Vestry of St. Luke's" March 28, 1882 (Letter was sent on April 12, 1882).
38.   M.D. Archives, April 22, 1882. Crummell was deeply upset because his opponents had taken

their complaints to local newspapers and tried to embarrass him in public.

39. Three voted for Crummell's resignation and two against. The dissenters (the chairman and the secretary of the committee) sent a separate letter to Bishop Pinkney indicating their desire that Dr. Crummell should be sustained. On April 3, 1882, a letter of support for Dr. Crummell signed by ninety-six "communicant members" (two signed their names by using X's) was sent to Bishop Pinkney. On April 19 and April 20, 1882, Langston W. Allen and John W. Cromwell sent additional letters of support to Bishop Pinkney (M.D. Archives).

40. M.D. Archives, May 2, 1882.

41. On Oct. 20, 1880 (M.D. Archives), the Vestry had complained in a letter to Bishop Pinkney that Crummell was planning a public concert at St. Luke's Church to raise funds for the church building. Bishop Pinkney replied on Oct. 30 that Crummell was acting in his right, for the church was not yet consecrated, and such matters were out of their jurisdiction. He expressed confidence that Crummell would not desecrate the church.

42. M.D. Archives, Feb. 6, 1883.

43. M.D. Archives, Vertical File, May 22, 1878; also, M.D. Archives, Sept. 25, 1878.

44. M.D. Archives, May 1878.

45. M.D. Archives, Vertical File, Dec. 19, 1878.

46. M.D. Archives, April 24, 1879.

47. M.D. Archives, Vertical File, Sept. 18, 1879 (Osmond St. James to Bishop Whittingham). One year later, a request was made to Bishop Pinkney to have St. James's license as a lay reader to Crummell revoked (Sept. 29, 1880).

48. M.D. Archives, Vertical File, May 1880.

49. M.D. Archives, Vertical File, June 22, 1880.

50. Meier, *Negro Thought* 50.

51. Cromwell's *History*, 133.
52. *A.C. Papers* 26 June 1894.
53. *A.C. Papers* 30 Nov. 1894.
54. *A.C. Papers* 24 Jan. 1895.
55. *A.C. Papers* 13 March 1895.
56. *A.C. Papers* 24 Jan. 1895.
57. *A.C. Papers* 13 March 1895.
58. "Social Principle" 290.
59. "Social Principle" 299.
60. W.E.B. Du Bois, *Black Reconstruction in America* (New York: Harcourt, Brace & Co., 1935) 271–274.
61. George M. Frederickson, *The Black Image in the White Mind* (New York: Harper and Row, 1971) 226–227.
62. "Social Principle" 303.
63. "The Black Woman of the South" 66.
64. "Storer Address" 31.
65. "The Black Woman of the South" 78.
66. "Social Principle" 309.
67. "The Race–Problem in America" 51.
68. "The Destined Superiority of the Negro" in *The Greatness of Christ and Other Sermons* 332–352.
69. "The Race–Problem in America" 48.
70. "Right–Mindedness" in *Africa and America* 375.
71. "Social Principle" 309.
72. *American Colonization Society Papers*, Letter to William Coppinger, April 23, 1874.
73. *Blyden* 39.
74. "The Race–Problem in America" 48.
75. "Social Principle" 296–297.
76. *John Bruce Papers* 22 March 1898.
77. *John Bruce Papers* 11 Nov. 1895.
78. "The Race–Problem in America" 50.
79. "Social Principle" 308.
80. "Storer Address" 22.
81. *John Bruce Papers* 30 Oct. 1896.
82. Aptheker, vol. 2, 649.
83. "The Dignity of Labor" 395–396.

84. *Francis J. Grimké Papers*, Folder 74, Sept. 11, 1889.
85. "The Race Problem in America" 51.
86. *John Bruce Papers* 30 Oct. 1896.
87. "Destined Superiority" 346.
88. "Destined Superiority" 351–352.
89. See *Negro Thought* chapter 1.
90. Benjamin Quarles and Leslie H. Fishel, eds. *The Black American: Documentary History* (Glenview, Ill.: Scott, Foresman, 1976) 315.
91. T. Thomas Fortune, *Black and White: Land, Labor, and Politics in the South* (1884; New York: Arno Press, 1969) 670–671. See also Emma Lou Thornbrough's *T. Thomas Fortune; Militant Journalist.* (Chicago: University of Chicago Press, 1972) passim.
92. *Black and White* 70.
93. *Black and White* 129.
94. Jubilate 24.
95. *John Bruce Papers*, n.d. However, the letter must have been written in the 1890s. On 27 Sept. 1897, for example, Crummell wrote to Bruce from England, referring to him (Fortune) as "a pitiful creature."
96. "Introduction" in *Africa and America* iv.
97. "Eulogium on Henry Highland Garnet" 291.
98. "Eulogium on Henry Highland Garnet" 291.
99. Black antagonism towards the Republican Party and Frederick Douglass continued to grow. For example, in 1882, at the state convention of Rhode Island, a critical attitude was expressed towards the Republican Party. Also, T. Thomas Fortune declaimed in *Black and White*: "I do not deem it binding upon colored men further to support the Republican Party " (670). These were open disavowals to Douglass's position. Even when Frederick Douglass had described himself as an "uneasy Republican," he was assailed by the black militant, John Bruce, as

being a traitor to the party that had steadfastly supported him. In short, Douglass was being assailed from all sides. When Douglass, after the death of his first wife Ana, married his white secretary Helen Pitts, in 1884, his credibility in the black community was at an all-time low.

100. Garnet, in deciding to go to Liberia, had complained to Crummell: "Would you have me . . . stay here [in America] and die among these ungrateful people?" ("Eulogium on Garnet" 303).

101. "Social Principle" 295.

102. Crummell had recently been to Liberia (1880) to receive the degree of Doctor of Laws from Liberia College, as recommended by Edward Blyden, the new president of the college (Lynch, Blyden 156). Crummell, during his visit, might have learned from Blyden about the still festering mulatto problem in Liberia (Lynch, Blyden 153 ff.), and Crummell probably wanted to spare Garnet the disappointment of caste prejudice in Africa.

103. *John Bruce Papers* 4 Nov. 1895.

104. *John Bruce Papers* 26 Nov. 1895.

105. *John Bruce Papers* 7 April 1896. On Nov. 7, 1897, Crummell reiterated to Bruce: "I am inclined to think we have a severe battle before us—a fight against caste in our own fold."

106. *John Bruce Papers* 10 March 1896. There was fierce animosity between Crummell and Fortune. In the newspaper, *Sun*, Fortune had accused the race-conscious Crummell of marrying a mulatto (his second wife). Crummell was very upset and wrote to Bruce about Fortune's "gross mendacity." As if trying to preserve his credibility, Crummell assured Bruce, "my wife is *not* a mulatto." *John Bruce Papers* 15 Dec. 1897.

107. *John Bruce Papers* 26 Nov. 1895.

108. *A.C. Papers*, Letter to Rev. Frazier Miller, June 19, 1894. Crummell had a cataract in one eye and lost sight in that eye for over seven years. Only when he went to England, after the inauguration of the American Negro Academy in 1897, did he have the cataract removed, and he wrote gleefully to Bruce, "Now I can see out of BOTH EYES." (*John Bruce Papers* 1 June 1897.)

109. *John Bruce Papers* 26 Nov. 1895.

110. *John Bruce Papers* 28 Feb. 1896.

111. *John Bruce Papers* 24 Dec. 1896.

112. *John Bruce Papers* 4 Nov. 1895.

113. *John Bruce Papers* 30 Oct. 1896.

114. *John Bruce Papers* 9 Dec. 1897.

115. *John Bruce Papers* 24 Dec. 1896.

116. *John Bruce Papers* 4 Feb. 1897.

117. *John Bruce Papers* 6 Dec. 1896.

118. *John Bruce Papers* 10 March 1896.

119. *John Bruce Papers* 24 Dec. 1896.

120. *John Bruce Papers* 22 March 1898.

121. Quoted in Cromwell's *History* 137–138.

122. *Civilization the Primal Need of the Race* 7.

123. *In Memoriam* 7.

124. *Francis J. Grimké Papers*, Folder 74, 40–2.

125. "Common Sense" 332.

126. "The Black Woman of the South" 79.

127. Davis, *This Is Liberia* 103.

128. "Excellence An End of the Trained Intellect" in *Africa and America* 347.

129. *A.C. Papers* 1 Nov. 1894.

130. Aptheker, vol. 2, 649.

131. "The Dignity of Labor" 400.

132. *Civilization the Primal Need of the Race* 14. Writing to Miller, Crummell stated: "A large class of our (so–called) white patrons . . . want a race of black boys, unthinking and uncultivated, to raise cotton, rice, tobacco." *A.C. Papers*, 28 July 1898.

133. *Civilization the Primal Need of the Race* 13.
134. *Civilization the Primal Need of the Race* 6.
135. Ferris 9.
136. Alfred Moss, Jr. in his study, *The American Negro Academy: Voice of the Talented Tenth*, attributes the idea of the Institute to R.R. Wright of Savannah, Georgia, who passed his idea to William Crogman of Atlanta, who in his turn got F. J. Grimké's interest in Washington, D.C. (19). Once Crummell became committed, he became the central figure (33). See also *Francis J. Grimké Papers*, William M. Crogman's letter to Grimké, Folder 74, Sept. 24, 1884.
137. Moss 24.
138. Moss 60.
139. *John Bruce Papers* Jan. 1898. See also Moss 32.
140. Moss 226.
141. Moss 54.
142. *A.C. Papers* 15 June 1897. Crummell also wrote to the Reverend Frazier Miller, "The American people care for nought save the *material* outcome of the Negro problem. The ideals of the Negro brain, life, character are a triviality." *A.C. Papers* 20 June 1898.
143. Cromwell's *History* 138.
144. *A.C. Papers* 30 June 1898.
145. "Common Sense" 341.
146. "The Dignity of Labor" 403.
147. "Excellence an End" 348.
148. "Storer Address" 33.
149. "Storer Address" 36.
150. "Address at the Laying of the Cornerstone" in *Africa and America* 462.
151. "Address at the Laying of the Cornerstone" 464.
152. Jubilate 25.
153. "Right–Mindedness" 373.
154. "Right–Mindedness" 366.
155. "Right–Mindedness" 369.

156. "Right–Mindedness" 372.
157. *Francis J. Grimké Papers*, Folder 74, June 30, 1886.
158. *In Memoriam* 7.
159. *A.C. Papers* 5 Oct. 1897.
160. "Storer Address" 22.
161. "Right–Mindedness" 374–376.
162. Jubilate 21.
163. Jubilate 20.
164. *John Cromwell Papers* 15 June 1897.
165. *In Memoriam* 7.
166. Cromwell's *History* 138.
167. Cromwell's *History* 138.
168. *John Cromwell's Papers* 3 Sept. 1898.
169. See an undated note in *A.C. Papers* (Reel 1, R1004).
170. *In Memoriam* 15.
171. *In Memoriam* 16.
172. Ferris 7.
173. *The Souls of Black Folk* 157.
174. *The Souls of Black Folk* 164.

Bibliography

MANUSCRIPT COLLECTIONS

Alexander Crummell Papers. Schomburg Collection, Harlem Branch of the New York Public Library, New York.

American Colonization Society Papers. Library of Congress, Washington, D.C. Includes Crummell correspondence.

John E. Bruce Papers. Schomburg Collection, Harlem Branch of the New York Public Library, New York. Includes Crummell correspondence.

Anna J. Cooper Papers. Manuscript Division, The Moorland–Spingarn Research Center, Howard University, Washington, D.C. Includes a Crummell entry in an autograph book.

John W. Cromwell Family Papers. Manuscript Division, The Moorland–Springarn Research Center, Howard University, Washington, D.C. Includes Crummell letters and items relating to Crummell.

Domestic and Foreign Missionary Society: Liberia Records. Archives of the Episcopal Church, Austin, Texas. Includes letters by and about Crummell.

Francis J. Grimké Papers. Manuscript Division, The Moorland–Springarn Research Center, Howard

University, Washington, D.C. Includes Crummell letters.

The Maryland Diocesan Archives, on deposit at the Maryland Historical Society, Baltimore, Maryland. Includes Crummell's correspondence, Bishop Whittingham's correspondence, and Bishop Whittingham's official journals and private diaries.

NEWSPAPERS

African Repository.
The Colored American (1837–1841).
Emancipator (1834).
North Star (1849).
The Weekly Anglo–African (1861–1862).

PUBLISHED MATERIALS

Akpan, Monday B. "Alexander Crummell and His African 'Race–Work': An Assessment of His Contributions in Liberia to Africa's 'Redemption,' 1853–1873," *Historical Magazine of the Protestant Episcopal Church* 46 (June 1977) 177–199.

Andrews, Charles. *History of New York African Free Schools.* New York: M. Day, 1830.

Aptheker, Herbert, ed. *A Documentary History of the Negro People in the United States.* 2 vols. Secaucus, New Jersey: Citadel Press, 1951.

Bell, Howard H. "The New Emigration Movement, 1849–1854: A Phase of Negro Nationalism," *Phylon* 20 (Summer 1959) 132–142.

–––. *A Survey of the Negro Convention Movement, 1830–1861.* New York: Arno Press, Inc., 1969.

Bell, Howard H., ed. *Minutes of the Proceedings of the National Negro Conventions, 1830–1864.* New York: Arno Press, Inc., 1969.

Billingsley, Andrew. *Black Families in White America*. Englewood Cliffs, New Jersey: Prentice-Hall, 1968.
Bracey, John H., August Meier, and Elliott Rudwick. *Black Nationalism in America*. New York: The Bobbs–Merrill Company, Inc., 1970.
Bragg, George F. *The Episcopal Church and the Black Man*. Baltimore: n.p. 1918.
——. *The First Negro Priest on Southern Soil*. Baltimore: The Church Advocate Print, 1909.
Brawley, Benjamin. *A Social History of the American Negro*. New York: Macmillan Co., 1921.
Brittan, Harriet G. *Scenes and Incidents of Every-Day Life in Africa*. 1860. New York: Negro University Press, 1969.
Brotz, Howard, ed. *Negro Social and Political Thought, 1850–1920*. New York: Basic Books, Inc., 1966.
Brown, William Wells. *The American Fugitive in Europe*. Boston: J. B. Jewett and Company, 1855.
——. *The Black Man: His Antecedents, His Genius, and His Achievements*. New York: T. Hamilton, 1863.
Churchman, *Caste and Slavery in the American Church*. New York: Wiley and Putnam, 1843.
Cromwell, John W. *The Negro in American History*. Washington, D.C.: The American Negro Academy, 1914.
Crummell, Alexander. *Africa and America*. 1891; New York: Negro Universities Press, 1969.
——. *Civilization the Primal Need of the Race*. Washington, D.C.: American Negro Academy, 1898.
——. *The Future of Africa*. 2d ed. New York: Charles Scribner, 1862.
——. *The Greatness of Christ and Other Sermons*. New York: T. Whittaker, 1882.
——. *The Shades and the Lights of a Fifty Years' Ministry*. Washington, D.C.: R.L. Pendleton, 1894.

Davis, Stanley. *This is Liberia.* New York: The William Frederick, Press, 1953.

Dorjahn, Vernon R. "The Changing Political System of the Temne," *Africa* 30 (April 1960) 109–140.

Drimmer, Melvin, ed. *Black History: A Reappraisal.* New York: Doubleday and Company, Inc., 1968.

Du Bois, W.E.B. *The Autobiography of W.E.B. Du Bois.* New York: International Publishers Co., Inc., 1968.

——. *Black Reconstruction in America.* New York: Harcourt, Brace and Co., 1935.

——. *The Philadelphia Negro.* 1899; New York: Schocken Books, 1967.

——. *The Souls of Black Folk.* 1903; Greenwich, Conn.: Fawcett Publications, Inc., 1961.

Ebony Magazine. *The Ebony Handbook.* Chicago: Johnson Publishing Company, Inc., 1974.

——. *The Negro Handbook.* Chicago: Johnson Publishing Company, Inc., 1966.

Ferris, William Henry. *Alexander Crummell, An Apostle of Negro Culture.* Washington, D.C.: American Negro Academy, 1920.

Fishel, Leslie H. and Benjamin Quarles, eds. *The Black American: Documentary History.* Glenview, Ill.: Scott, Foresman, 1976.

Foner, Philip. *Business and Slavery.* Chapel Hill: The University of North Carolina Press, 1941.

Foner, Philip, ed. *The Voice of Black America.* New York: Capricorn Books, 1975.

Fortune, T. Thomas. *Black and White: Land, Labor, and Politics in the South.* 1884; New York: Arno Press, 1969.

Foster, Charles. "The Colonization of Free Negroes in Liberia, 1816–1835," *Journal of Negro History* 38 (Jan. 1953) 41–66.

Fox, Earl Lee. *The American Colonization Society, 1817–1840.* Baltimore: The John Hopkins University Press, 1919.

Franklin, John H. *Reconstruction After the Civil War*. Chicago: The University of Chicago Press, 1961.

Frazier, E. Franklin. *The Negro Family*. New York: Dryden Press, 1948.

Fredrickson, George M. *The Black Image in the White Mind*. New York: Harper and Row, 1971.

Fyfe, C. H. *A History of Sierra Leone*. London: Oxford University Press, 1962.

Garrison, William Lloyd. *Selections from the Writings and Speeches of William Lloyd Garrison*. 1852; New York: The New American Library, Inc., 1969.

Gross, Bella. "Freedom's Journal," *Journal of Negro History* 17 (July 1932) 241–286.

Harris, Sheldon H. *Paul Cuffe: Black America and the African Return*. New York: Simon and Schuster, 1972.

Haswell, Charles H. *Reminiscences of an Octogenarian*. New York: Harper and Brothers, 1896.

Hayson, Walter B. "Eulogy," *The Church Standard* 14 Jan. 1899: 355–356.

Holden, Edith. *Blyden of Liberia*. New York: Vantage Press, 1966.

Legum, Colin. *Pan-Africanism*. New York: Frederick A. Praeger Publishers, 1965.

Lindsay, Arnett G. "The Economic Condition of the Negroes of New York Prior to 1861," *Journal of Negro History* 6 (April 1921) 190–199.

Litwack, Leon. *North of Slavery*. Chicago: The University of Chicago Press, 1966.

Logan, Rayford. *The Negro in American Life and Thought: The Nadir, 1877–1901*. (1954; published as *The Betrayal of the Negro, From Hayes to Wilson*, New York: Collier Books, 1965).

Lynch, Hollis. *Edward Wilmot Blyden*. New York: Oxford University Press, 1967.

Lynch, Hollis, ed. *Selected Letters of Edward Wilmot Blyden*. Millwood, New York: KTO Press,

1978.

Mason, Julian D., ed. *The Poems of Phillis Wheatley*. Chapel Hill: The University of North Carolina Press, 1966.

Meier, August. *The Making of Black America*. New York: Atheneum, 1971.

———. *Negro Thought in America, 1880–1915*. Ann Arbor: University of Michigan Press, 1963.

Meier, August and Elliott Rudwick. *From Plantation to Ghetto*. Rev. ed. New York: Hill and Wang, 1970.

Miller, Floyd. *The Search for a Black Nationality: Black Emigration and Colonization*. Urbana: University of Illinois Press, 1975.

Minutes of Massachusetts Colonization Society. May 28, 1862.

Moses, Wilson Jeremiah. "Alexander Crummell: Civilizing Missionary," *Journal of Negro History* 60 (April 1975) 229–251.

———. *The Golden Age of Black Nationalism, 1850–1925*. Hamden, Conn.: The Shoe String Press, 1978.

Moss, Alfred, Jr. *The American Negro Academy: Voice of the Talented Tenth*. Baton Rouge: Louisiana State University Press, 1981.

Nesbit, William. *Four Months in Liberia*. Pittsburgh: J.T. Shryock, 1855.

Painter, Nell Irbin. *Exodusters: Black Migration to Kansas After Reconstruction*. New York: Knopf, 1976.

Payne, A. H. "The Negro in New York Prior to 1860," *The Howard Review* 1 (June 1923) 1–64.

Payne, Daniel A. *Recollection of Seventy Years*. 1891; New York: Arno Press, Inc., 1968.

Pease, Jane H. and William H. Pease. "Black Power—The Debate in 1840," *Phylon* 29 (Spring 1968) 19–26.

Phillips, Henry L. *In Memoriam of the Late Rev. Alexander Crummell*. Philadelphia: Coleman, 1899.

Porter, Dorothy, ed. *Early Negro Writing*. Boston:

Beacon Press, 1971.

Quarles, Benjamin. "Ministers Without Portfolio," *Journal of Negro History* 39 (Jan. 1954), 27–42.

---. *The Negro in the Civil War.* Boston: Little, Brown and Company, 1953.

Redkey, Edwin S. *Black Exodus: Black Nationalist and Back-to-Africa Movements, 1890–1910.* New Haven: Yale University Press, 1969.

Ripley, C. Peter, ed. *The Black Abolitionist Papers.* 1 vol. to date. Chapel Hill: The University of North Carolina Press, 1985– .

St. Luke's Episcopal Church: One Hundred Years. Washington, D.C.: The Church, 1973.

Scruggs, Otey M. *We the Children of Africa in This Land: Alexander Crummell.* Washington, D.C.: Howard University Press, 1972.

Shepperson, George. "Frederick Douglass and Scotland," *Journal of Negro History* 38 (July 1953) 307–321.

Sherwood, Henry N. "Paul Cuffe," *Journal of Negro History* 8 (April 1923) 153–229.

Smith, James McCune. "Introduction" in Henry Highland Garnet's *A Memorial Discourse.* Philadelphia: J.M. Wilson, 1865.

Stampp, Kenneth and Leon F. Litwack, eds. *Reconstruction: An Anthology of Revisionist Writings.* Baton Rouge: Louisiana State University Press, 1969.

Staudenraus, P.J. *The American Colonization Movement, 1816–1865.* New York: Columbia University Press, 1961.

Tappan, Arthur. *The Life of Arthur Tappan.* New York: Hurd, 1870.

Thompson, Mary. *The Colored Home in the City of New York.* New York: John F. Trow, 1851.

Thornbrough, Emma Lou. *T. Thomas Fortune, Militant Journalist.* Chicago: The University of Chicago Press, 1972.

Wesley, Charles H. "The Negro of New York in the

Emancipation Movement," *Journal of Negro History* 24 (Jan. 1939) 65–103.

Whale, Kathleen O. "Alexander Crummell: Black Evangelist and Pan–Negro Nationalist," *Phylon* 29 (Winter 1968) 388–395.

Williams, Eric. *Capitalism and Slavery.* 1944; New York: G.P. Putnam's Sons, 1966.

Williams, Peter, Jr. *Discourse Delivered on the Death of Captain Paul Cuffe.* New York: B. Young and Co., 1817.

Williams, Samuel. *A Sketch of the Life of the Rev. Samuel Williams.* Philadelphia: King and Baird, 1857.

Woodson, Carter G. *Free Negro Heads of Families in the United States in 1830.* Washington, D.C.: The Association for the Study of Negro Life and History, Inc., 1925.

———. *Negro Orators and Their Orations.* Washington, D.C.: The Associated Publishers, Inc., 1925.

Woodson, Carter G., ed. *The Mind of the Negro as Reflected in Letters Written During the Crisis, 1800–1860.* Washington, D.C.: The Association for the Study of Negro Life and History, Inc., 1926.

Yates, William. *Rights of Colored Men.* Philadelphia: Merrihew and Gunn, 1838.

UNPUBLISHED DISSERTATIONS

Fox, Ronald N. "The Reverend Alexander Crummell: An Apostle of Black Culture." Unpublished B.S.T. Thesis, General Theological Seminary, 1969.

Sekey, Benedict. "A History of Liberia College." Unpublished Master's Thesis, Howard University, 1973.

Taylor, Olive. "The Protestant Episcopal Church and the Negro in Washington, D.C." Unpublished doctoral dissertation, Howard University, 1973.

Index

sickness, 29, 68–69, 126, 132, 134, 162, 212n; *conflicts*: Blyden, 128–131, 153; Douglass, 45, 160; Fortune, 158–159, 162, 211n; Liberia College, 121–122, 126; mulattoes, 87, 119–123, 126, 144, 153–154, 155, 173–175; Onderdonk, 26–28, 191n; Payne, 79–92; son, 89–92; vestry, 144–148, 208n; *education*: African Free School, 20–21; Cambridge University, 58–59; Noyes Academy, 22–24; Oneida Institute, 24–25, 190–191n; *friends*: Blyden, 130–131; Garnet, 1–2, 13–14, 19, 20, 22–24, 109, 114–115, 135, 161; Sidney, 20, 22–25, 29, 30; Dunbar, 157, 162, 163, 166, 176–177; *ideas*: on Africanness, 7–8; on Afro–American rights, 8; on black education, 41–48, 165–167, 170–171; on black leadership, 159–164; on the black masses, 40–41, 76, 150–159, 163–164; on black self–help, 140–144, 157; on "double–consciousness," 14–15; on Pan–Africanism, xiii, xiv–xv, 4, 5, 10, 15, 52–53, 60–66, 69–70, 73, 76, 77, 78, 85, 92, 93, 96, 97, 98, 100–101, 103–104, 105, 111, 112, 115–116, 119, 120, 133, 139, 144, 149, 152, 165, 175; on philosophical framework, 31–41; on political philosophy, 72–73; on race, 1, 5, 37–38, 64–65, 97–98, 99–100, 103, 152–153, 175–176; on Talented Tenth, 39–41, 150, 167; on women, 2–3, 116, 165; *influences*: father, 1–2; mother, 2–3; Peter Williams, 4–10; *setbacks*: dismissal from Foreign Mission, 74–75; dismissal from Liberia College, 122, 123; finances, 24, 74, 85–86, 107–108, 131,

195n; *undertakings*: ANA, 167–170; the erecting of Trinity Church (Liberia), 73–75; the erecting of St. Luke's (Wash., D.C.), 140–149; fund–raising in England, 55, 57–58; fund–raising in U.S., 143; recruitment of Afro–Americans, 108, 110–119. *Works*: "The Black Woman of the South," 116, 167, 181; "Common Sense in Common Schooling," 167; "Defense of the Negro Race," 156; "The Dignity of Labor," 166; "Divorce," 88; "The English Language in Liberia," 111; "Eulogium on the Life and Character of Thomas Clarkson," 50; "Eulogy on the Life and Character of Thomas Simpkins Sidney," 30; "Excellence, an End of the Trained Intellect," 167; "Existence and Essence of God," 49; "The Law of Liberty," 48, 55; "Lecture on the Lord's Prayer," 55; "The Need of New Ideas and New Aims for a New Era," 160; "The Negro Race Not Under a Curse," 62; "The Social Principle," 141, 154; "Thy Kingdom Come," 49
Crummell, Boston, 1, 5, 10, 12, 14, 17, 186n
Crummell, Charles, 147, 178
Crummell, Jennie Morris (second wife), 139, 177
Crummell, Mrs. Boston (Charity Hicks), 3
Crummell, Sidney, 89–92, 108, 126, 131, 137, 138, 147, 178, 180, 181
Crummell Memorial, 181
Cuffe, Paul, 5–7, 10, 56, 187n
Cyprian, 66

About the Author

GREGORY U. RIGSBY is Professor of English Studies at the University of the District of Columbia. He has written articles in the fields of Afro-American Studies and Caribbean Literature for numerous journals, including *CLA Journal, Journal of Negro Education, Journal of Western Studies,* and *Philosophical Forum.*

Recent Titles in
Contributions in Afro-American and African Studies
Series Advisers: John W. Blassingame and Henry Louis Gates, Jr.

Black Theatre in the 1960s and 1970s: A Historical-Critical Analysis of the Movement
Mance Williams

An Old Creed for the New South: Proslavery Ideology and Historiography, 1865-1918
John David Smith

Wilson Harris and the Modern Tradition: A New Architecture of the World
Sandra E. Drake

Portrait of an Expatriate: William Gardner Smith, Writer
LeRoy S. Hodges, Jr.

Race, Politics, and Culture: Critical Essays on the Radicalism of the 1960s
Adolph Reed, Jr.

The White Press and Black America
Carolyn Martindale

Africa and the West: The Legacies of Empire
Isaac James Mowoe and Richard Bjornson, editors

A Black Elite: A Profile of Graduates of UNCF Colleges
Daniel C. Thompson

"De Lawd": Richard B. Harrison and *The Green Pastures*
Walter C. Daniel

Health Care Issues in Black America: Policies, Problems, and Prospects
Woodrow Jones, Jr., and Mitchell F. Rice, editors

The Character of the Word: The Texts of Zora Neale Hurston
Karla F. C. Holloway

Surprizing Narrative: Olaudah Equiano and the Beginnings of Black Autobiography
Angelo Costanzo

Conscientious Sorcerers: The Black Postmodernist Fiction of LeRoi Jones/Amiri Baraka, Ishmael Reed, and Samuel R. Delany
Robert Elliot Fox